My Google Chromebook™

Second Edition

Michael Miller

800 East 96th Street,
Indianapolis, Indiana 46240 USA

My Google Chromebook™, Second Edition

Copyright © 2013 by Pearson Education, Inc.

ISBN-13: 978-0-7897-5138-6
ISBN-10: 0-7897-5138-0

Library of Congress Cataloging-in-Publication Data is on file.

Printed in the United States of America

Second Printing: November 2013

Trademarks

All terms mentioned in this book that are known to be trademarks or service marks have been appropriately capitalized. Que Publishing cannot attest to the accuracy of this information. Use of a term in this book should not be regarded as affecting the validity of any trademark or service mark.

Warning and Disclaimer

Every effort has been made to make this book as complete and as accurate as possible, but no warranty or fitness is implied. The information provided is on an "as is" basis. The author and the publisher shall have neither liability nor responsibility to any person or entity with respect to any loss or damages arising from the information contained in this book.

Bulk Sales

Que Publishing offers excellent discounts on this book when ordered in quantity for bulk purchases or special sales. For more information, please contact

U.S. Corporate and Government Sales

1-800-382-3419

corpsales@pearsontechgroup.com

For sales outside of the U.S., please contact

International Sales

international@pearsoned.com

Editor-in-Chief
Greg Wiegand

Acquisitions Editor
Rick Kughen

Development Editor
Charlotte Kughen
The Wordsmithery LLC

Managing Editor
Sandra Schroeder

Project Editor
Mandie Frank

Indexer
Cheryl Lenser

Proofreader
Sarah Kearns

Technical Editor
Karen Weinstein

Publishing Coordinator
Kristin Watterson

Designer
Anne Jones

Compositor
Tricia Bronkella

Contents at a Glance

My Google Chromebook™, Second Edition

Table of Contents

11   **Using Chrome Apps and Extensions**   **161**

13   Printing with Google Cloud Print   205

14   Using Google Chrome Safely and Securely   215

My Google Chromebook™, Second Edition

About the Author

Michael Miller is a prolific and popular writer of more than 100 non-fiction books, known for his ability to explain complex topics to everyday readers. He writes about a variety of topics, including technology, business, and music. His best-selling books for Que include *Absolute Beginner's Guide to Computer Basics, Easy Computer Basics, Using Google Advanced Search, Your First Notebook PC, Facebook for Grown-Ups,* and *My Pinterest.* Worldwide, his books have sold more than 1 million copies.

Find out more at the author's website: **www.molehillgroup.com**

Follow the author on Twitter: **molehillgroup**

Dedication

To my wonderful grandkids Alethia, Collin, Hayley, Judah, and Lael.

Acknowledgments

Thanks to all the folks at Que who helped turned this manuscript into a book, including Rick Kughen, Greg Wiegand, Charlotte Kughen, and technical editor Karen Weinstein.

We Want to Hear from You!

As the reader of this book, you are our most important critic and commentator. We value your opinion and want to know what we're doing right, what we could do better, what areas you'd like to see us publish in, and any other words of wisdom you're willing to pass our way.

We welcome your comments. You can email or write to let us know what you did or didn't like about this book—as well as what we can do to make our books better.

Please note that we cannot help you with technical problems related to the topic of this book.

When you write, please be sure to include this book's title and author as well as your name and email address. We will carefully review your comments and share them with the author and editors who worked on the book.

Email: feedback@quepublishing.com

Mail: Que Publishing
         ATTN: Reader Feedback
         800 East 96th Street
         Indianapolis, IN 46240 USA

Reader Services

Visit our website and register this book at www.quepublishing.com/register for convenient access to any updates, downloads, or errata that might be available for this book.

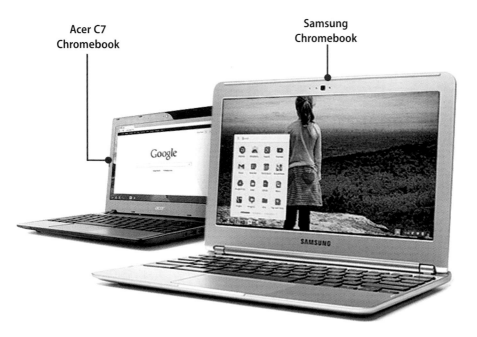

Acer C7
Chromebook

Samsung
Chromebook

In this chapter, you get an introduction to web-based computing with Google's Chrome OS running on Chromebook and Chromebox computers.

→ What Is a Chromebook?
→ What Is a Chromebox?
→ What Is Google Chrome OS?
→ What Is Cloud Computing?
→ Should You Buy a Chromebook?
→ Which Chromebook Should You Buy?

Understanding Chrome, Chromebooks, and Cloud Computing

A Chromebook is a new breed of ultra-portable netbook computer—kind of like a tablet PC but with a keyboard. They're lightweight and have very long battery life, and with one you can do all your computing from wherever you have an Internet connection.

Chromebooks run the Google Chrome operating system (also known as Chrome OS), a new type web-based operating system. They can run any web-based application. Everything a Chromebook does is a form of cloud computing, which uses applications and data files stored in the "cloud" of the Internet, not on any individual personal computer.

Because of its web-based nature, using a Chromebook and the Chrome OS is quite a bit different from using a traditional notebook PC and either Microsoft Windows or the Mac OS. To get the most use out of your new Chromebook, then, you need to become familiar with how cloud computing works—as well as all the ins and outs of your new Chromebook.

What Is a Chromebook?

Put simply, a Chromebook is a netbook computer that runs the Google Chrome OS. A netbook is a particularly small and lightweight type of notebook PC; whereas most netbooks run a version of the Microsoft Windows operating system, Chromebooks instead run Google's web-based operating system. (Hence the name Chromebook—a netbook running Google Chrome OS.)

Like all netbooks, a Chromebook is smaller and lighter than a traditional notebook PC. Because most Chromebooks don't contain a hard disk or CD/DVD drive, that space and weight is removed from the equation. Most Chromebooks have 12" (or so) diagonal screens, are very thin, and weigh less than three pounds.

If there's no hard drive inside, how does a Chromebook store your data? The answer is *solid state storage*, the same kind you find on USB flash drives and the memory cards you use with your digital camera. Most current Chromebooks come with 16GB of internal solid state storage—considerably less than what you find with a traditional notebook, but it's all that Chrome OS needs to run. As for storing your data, that's what the Web is for; a Chromebook needs only minimal local storage.

Exceptions

The one exception to the no-hard drive rule is Acer's C7 Chromebook, which comes with a 320GB hard drive for local storage—even though you can still use cloud storage for your data, if you like. And the singular exception to the 12" screen size is HP's Pavilion Chromebook, which has a 14" screen.

In terms of processing power, today's Chromebooks use one of two dual-core processors. Acer, HP, and Lenovo models use an Intel Celeron processor; the Samsung Chromebook opts for a proprietary Samsung Exynos 5 Dual processor. To be honest, these aren't the most powerful processors available today, but they're all that's needed to run the small-footprint Chrome OS.

This combination of small screen, minimal solid state storage, and efficient processor means that a Chromebook has an impressive battery life—anywhere from 6 to 8 hours on a charge. (Less for the Acer model with a built-in hard drive and the HP with the larger screen; both of these units get only 4 hours or so of battery life.) Chromebooks are also virtually instant on; most boot up in 10 seconds or so, and resume instantly from sleep mode. It's a much different—and much more efficient—computing experience than what you're used to.

In essence, then, a Chromebook is a computer that is built and optimized for the Web, using Chrome OS. It provides a faster, simplified, and more secure computing environment than with traditional Windows or Mac computers.

Chromebooks Online

Learn more about Chromebooks and Google Chrome OS online at www.google.com/chromebook/.

What Is a Chromebox?

Chromebooks aren't the only devices that run Google's Chrome operating system. If you want a Chrome computer in a traditional desktop form factor, check out Samsung's Chromebox—a small device that's perfect as the base unit for a desktop PC system.

A Chromebox is merely a Chromebook without a screen or keyboard. It's a small box you can hold in your hand, but it has enough inputs and outputs to connect an external monitor, keyboard, and mouse—and thus create a Chrome-based desktop PC.

As such, a Chromebox is ideal for companies wishing to replace existing Windows-based desktop PCs. It's a perfect choice for organizations that have standardized on the Google Apps suite of applications. Like portable Chromebooks, Chromeboxes run Google's Chrome operating system.

What Is Google Chrome OS?

We've talked a lot about the Chrome operating system that runs on Chromebook and Chromebox devices. But what exactly is the Chrome OS?

Google's Chrome OS is the world's first operating system for the new era of cloud computing. It's a web-based operating system in that it relies on a variety of web-based services and applications to work; it doesn't run traditional desktop applications. It's designed to be used on smallish computers, such as the portable Chromebook and living room–based Chromebox, that are wirelessly connected to the Internet.

Because it runs over the Web, Chrome OS is a "lightweight" operating system, meaning it doesn't have a large footprint in terms of file size or memory or processing requirements. It can fit quite easily within the limited internal storage space of a small Chromebook or Chromebox computer, and it is automatically updated whenever the computer is connected to the Internet. It's also relatively fast and efficient, which results in short startup times and sprightly operation.

Chrome and Linux

Chrome is an open source operating system, which means that it can be freely distributed without paying expensive licensing costs. It is based on a version of Linux, another operating system that itself is based on the established UNIX operating system. The Chrome OS interface runs on top of the underlying Linux kernel.

The first iteration of Chrome OS closely resembled Google's Chrome web browser. There was no traditional desktop, as is found in Microsoft Windows or Apple's Mac OS, and applications were launched in individual tabs within the Chrome browser. Using this early version of Chrome was more like browsing the Web than it was navigating a complex operating system, such as Windows.

The initial version of Chrome OS; no desktop, just a single browser with multiple tabs.

People didn't like that browser-based interface, so Google changed it. The current version of Chrome OS features the same sort of desktop you find in Windows or the Mac OS. Applications open in their own multiple windows on the desktop, and you can easily switch from one open window to another. It's very similar to using Microsoft Windows or the Mac OS; the big difference is that most of what you launch is housed on the Web, not locally.

The current version of Chrome OS, complete with traditional desktop and multiple windows.

That's right, Chrome OS does not and cannot run traditional software programs; everything it runs must be a web-based application. This means that you can't use programs like Microsoft Office or Adobe Photoshop.

That's not necessarily a bad thing. Using web-based applications—or what we call *cloud computing*—has a lot of benefits, as we'll discuss next.

What Is Cloud Computing?

Cloud computing represents a major shift in how we run computer applications and store data. With cloud computing, instead of hosting applications and data on an individual desktop computer, everything is hosted in the "cloud"—a nebulous assemblage of computers and servers accessed via the

Internet. Cloud computing lets you access your applications and documents from anywhere in the world, freeing you from the confines of the desktop and facilitating wholesale group collaboration.

How Traditional Desktop Computing Works

Traditional desktop computing is all about the sovereignty of the individual computer. Although individual computers can be networked together, all the computer power resides on the desktop; each personal computer has its own massive amounts of memory and hard disk storage.

This storage is put to good use for storing all your programs and data. You have to install on your computer a copy of each software program you use. These programs are run from your computer's hard drive, and the documents you create are stored on the same computer and hard drive. Programs and documents are specific to individual machines.

In other words, desktop computing is computer-centric.

How Cloud Computing Works

In contrast, cloud computing doesn't depend on individual computers much at all. With cloud computing, the applications you run and the documents you create aren't stored on your personal computer, but are instead stored on servers that you access via the Internet. If your computer crashes, the application is still available for others to use—or for you to run from another computer.

It's the same thing with the documents you create, but even more so. Because the documents are stored in the "cloud," anyone with permission can not only access the documents but can also edit and collaborate on those documents in real time.

Unlike traditional computing, then, this cloud computing model isn't computer-centric, it's user- or document-centric. Which computer you use to access a document simply isn't important; instead, the focus is on your apps and data, which you can access from anywhere, on any device—such as a Chromebook or Chromebox PC.

DEFINING THE CLOUD

Key to the definition of cloud computing is the "cloud" itself. Put simply, the cloud is a grid of interconnected computers. These computers can be personal computers or network servers; they can be public or private.

For example, Google hosts a cloud that consists of both smallish PCs and larger servers. Google's cloud is a private one (that is, Google owns it) that is publicly accessible (by Google's users).

This cloud of computers extends beyond a single company or enterprise. The applications and data served by the cloud are available to a broad group of users, cross-enterprise and cross-platform. Access is via the Internet; any authorized user can access these docs and apps from any computer over any Internet connection. And, to the user, the technology and infrastructure behind the cloud is invisible; all you see are the applications and documents you use, not the technology that drives access.

Should You Buy a Chromebook?

Chromebooks and Chromeboxes both define and depend on the concept of cloud computing. All the apps you run and all the files you create are stored on the Web and accessed via the Internet on your Google Chrome device.

But Chromebooks and Chromeboxes aren't the only type of computing devices that rely on cloud computing. Smartphones and tablets are much like Chromebooks (but without the keyboard) in that they have minimal internal storage because they store most of their data on the Web. Although these devices might store many of their apps locally, there's still a lot of cloud streaming going on.

For this reason, people use Chromebooks for many of the same tasks they do on their iPads or other tablets. Watching streaming video from the cloud is a snap with a Chromebook, as is listening to streaming music, viewing your Facebook or Twitter feed, and the like. The fact that you have a keyboard attached just makes the Chromebook that much more versatile.

This begs the question—is a Chromebook the right device for you? Or should you invest in a tablet, or a traditional PC?

As with any technology purchase, you need to weigh the pros and cons and then decide what's best for your personal use. With that in mind, let's take a look at the benefits and disadvantages you might find in using a Chromebook running Chrome OS.

Chromebook Versus Tablet

For many users, a Chromebook is a viable alternative to purchasing an iPad or similar tablet computer. There are many advantages to using a Chromebook over a tablet, including the following:

- **Keyboard and touchpad**—A tablet is just a screen—a touchscreen, mind you, but a screen nonetheless. If you want to do anything beyond watching movies and browsing web pages, it's difficult; you have to tap an onscreen virtual keyboard, which isn't that great for anything more than a tweet or a short Facebook post. A Chromebook, on the other hand, includes a traditional computer keyboard and mouse-like touch-pad, both of which are necessary if you need to input much of anything at all. Given the similar price, that keyboard and touchpad add tremen-dous value to a Chromebook.

- **More productivity**—The Chromebook's keyboard and mouse input let you be a lot more productive than you can on a tablet. Whether you're writing school essays or business reports, you need that keyboard. Same thing if you do a lot of emailing or number crunching; you just can't do it as well or as accurately on a tablet's onscreen keyboard. The touchpad is also useful if you're doing heavy-duty photo editing or serious game play. In other words, if it's productivity you're looking for, a Chromebook is the way to go.

- **Inputs and outputs**—Some tablets have a USB port or two, but many (including the best-selling Apple iPad) don't. That's where a Chromebook shines. In terms of connectors, it's outfitted like a traditional notebook PC. There are some differences between models, but expect to find at least two USB input/output ports and an HDMI output. The USB ports let you connect USB flash drives, external storage devices, and peripherals; the HDMI port provides high definition audio/video output to a wide-screen TV or home theater system. You don't get all this with a typical tablet.

- **Bigger screen**—Tablets today come in two primary screen sizes—small (8" or so) and large (10" or so). Small tablets typically cost about the same as a Chromebook, in the $200 to $250 range, but with a much smaller screen. And the larger tablets, while much more expensive, aren't that much larger—and their screens are still smaller than a Chromebook screen. If you need the screen real estate, whether for watching movies or browsing websites, the Chromebook is the choice for you.

- **Price**—Starting at $199, Chromebooks are price-competitive with the lower-end tablets, such as the small-screen Google Nexus 7 and Amazon Kindle Fire HD. Even the higher-priced Chromebooks are considerably lower-priced than even the lowest-price Apple iPad. The price comparison is even more compelling when you realize that for the price of an iPad ($500 and up), you can buy *two* Chromebooks—or just one and have money left over for other fun stuff.

In other words, a Chromebook gives you all the productivity and connectivity of a notebook computer, but in a tablet-like form factor and price point. If you're comparing a Chromebook to a tablet, you can do a lot more with the Chromebook.

Chromebook Versus Traditional Notebook

A Chromebook is also a viable alternative to a traditional Windows or Mac notebook PC. There are a lot of advantages to the Chromebook in this comparison, including the following:

- **Low price**—Today's third-generation Chromebooks cost between $200 and $400—much lower priced than traditional notebook PCs, which are likely to set you back $500 or more. (Much more, in the terms of Apple products.) When you want a second device for consuming media or casual productivity, the low cost of a Chromebook is very appealing.

First-Generation Chromebooks

The initial round of Chromebooks, released in 2011, were not as appealing, price-wise. Those Chromebooks sold for $350 to $500, and didn't represent as good a value compared to tablets or traditional notebook PCs.

- **No software to buy**—Not only does a Chromebook cost less than a comparable notebook PC, you also don't have to lay out big bucks for software to run on the device. Because a Chromebook doesn't run traditional (and expensive) computer software, you instead load a variety of free or low-cost web-based apps. Considering the high price of Microsoft Office and similar programs, you can save hundreds or even thousands of dollars by using web-based applications instead. That also means you don't have to worry about installing multiple programs, or managing regular upgrades; with web apps, there's nothing to install, and all upgrades happen automatically.

- **No worry about local storage and backup**—With a traditional computer, you have to manage limited hard disk storage space and worry about backing up your important files. Not so with a Chromebook; all your files are stored on the Web, where you have virtually unlimited storage, so you don't have to worry about data storage at all. You also don't have to worry about backups because you always have a copy of your files online.

- **Reduced malware danger**—Because you don't download and run traditional computer software, computer viruses and spyware are virtual non-issues on a Chromebook. You don't even have to run antivirus programs because viruses simply can't be installed on Chrome OS.

- **Enhanced security**—If you lose a traditional computer, all your personal files and information is also lost—or, in the case of theft, placed in the hands of criminals. Not so with a Chromebook. If somebody steals your Chromebook, all they get is a piece of hardware; because all files and data are stored on the Web, nothing important resides on the machine itself. This makes a Chromebook the most secure computer today.

- **More portability**—Like a tablet, a Chromebook is smaller and lighter than a traditional notebook PC. That's great for when you're on the go.

- **Faster boot up**—Instant resumption from sleep mode. Reboot from scratch in less than 10 seconds, on average. Try to find a Windows-based computer that can do that.

- **Enhanced collaboration**—Cloud computing is built for collaboration. Because your documents are all stored on the Web, multiple users can access and edit those documents in real time. No more passing files around from user to user—all you have to do is use your Chromebook to go online and start collaborating.

- **Ideal for multiple users**—With traditional computing, every user has to have his own computer, which stores all his files and personalized computing environment. With Chrome OS, your files, applications, and personalized desktop are stored on the Web; any Chromebook you use becomes your personal Chromebook after you log into your Google Account. A single Chromebook can easily be shared between multiple users, and it really doesn't matter whose computer it is.

Put simply, a Chromebook gives you all the advantages of a tablet combined with traditional notebook PC productivity—at a very attractive price. A Chromebook is smaller, lighter, faster, and more secure than a Windows or Mac notebook, and costs a lot less, too.

Chromebooks in Schools

Chromebooks have proved particularly popular in the education market. The low hardware cost, coupled with less need for expensive software and easier maintenance, have encouraged many schools to standardize on Chromebooks for their students.

What's Not to Like?

Whether you're in the market for a tablet or notebook computer, a Chromebook certainly sounds like a contender for your purchase dollars. But Chromebooks aren't for everyone; there are some limitations in using a Chromebook for your computing and web surfing. In particular, consider the following:

- **You need an Internet connection.** Because Chrome OS is a web-based operating system, a Chromebook is virtually useless if you can't connect to the Internet. You use the Internet to connect to both your applications and documents, so if you don't have an Internet connection, you can't access anything, even your own documents. A dead Internet connection means no work, period—and, in areas where Internet connections are few or inherently unreliable, this could be a deal breaker. When you're offline, a Chromebook really can't do anything.

Working Offline

Some web-based applications, such as Google Docs and Gmail, have offline modes that let you continue working without an Internet connection. Most other apps, however, need to be connected to run. (And, naturally, you need an Internet connection to view or listen to streaming media, and to browse the Web.)

- **Doesn't work well with slow connections.** Similarly, a low-speed Internet connection, such as that found with old school dial-up services, makes using a Chromebook painful at best and often impossible. Web-based apps often require a lot of bandwidth to download, as do streaming movies and music. If you're laboring with a low-speed dial-up connection, it might take seemingly forever just to change from page to page in a document, let alone use a streaming audio or video service. In other words, using a Chromebook isn't for the slow or broadband-impaired.

- **You can't use traditional software.** There are lots of free or low-cost web-based applications available, but not all the programs you currently use have web-based counterparts. For example, if you do a lot of photo editing, you'd be hard pressed to find a web application with all the functionality of Adobe Photoshop. Even those apps that have web-based versions, such as Microsoft Office, often offer less functionality and compatibility online. Make sure that you can do what you need to do totally over the Web before you make the jump to a Chromebook.

- **Is cloud-based data really secure?** With cloud computing, all your data is stored on the cloud. That's all well and good, but how secure is the cloud? Can other, unauthorized users gain access to your confidential data? These are important questions, and well worth further examination. If you're worried about data security or reliability, using Chrome OS might not be for you.

And when you're comparing a Chromebook with a tablet PC, consider the following issues:

- **It's heavier than a tablet.** Although a Chromebook is a very light notebook PC, it's still a little heavier than a tablet. The Samsung Chromebook comes in at 2.4 pounds, which is about a pound more than the iPad.

(Other models are even heavier; the Acer C7 weighs a tad over 3 pounds, and both the HP Pavilion and Lenovo Chromebooks are closer to 4 pounds.) If weight matters, a tablet might be more appealing.

- **It has a shorter battery life than a tablet.** The 4-to-6 hour battery life of a third-generation Chromebook sounds good compared to the battery life of a typical notebook PC, but is somewhat shorter than what you get with most current tablets. For example, Apple's iPad 4 boasts a 10-hour battery life, which is nothing to sneeze at.

What Chromebook Should You Buy?

If you've read this far, I'll assume that you're still interested in purchasing a new Chromebook computer. The next question is a simple one—what models are available?

The first generation of Google Chromebooks launched back in 2011. These were more expensive units, running anywhere from $349 to $499. As you might suspect, that pricing made them less than stellar performers in the marketplace.

In mid-2012, Samsung introduced two second-generation Chromebook models, priced at $449 and $549. Despite display and keyboard improvements, these models were viewed as too expensive and generally ignored by consumers.

That all changed in October of 2012, when the third generation of Chromebooks hit the market—and were an immediate hit with consumers. Not only was Chrome OS itself improved over the initial version, but these new Chromebooks—from Acer and Samsung—offered a lot more bang for the buck. With pricing starting as low as $199, Chromebooks suddenly became a lot more attractive, especially for users looking for a second computer-like device for casual use. In fact, these new Chromebooks were so popular that they sold out well before Christmas, and the Samsung Chromebook was Amazon.com's best-selling notebook PC of the holiday season.

The lowest-priced third-generation Chromebook is the 11.6" Acer C7, priced at $199.99. It comes in an iron gray finish and offers 2GB memory and a 320GB hard drive for internal storage. It offers Wi-Fi wireless connectivity and a built-in webcam, and weighs just a hair more than 3 pounds.

Acer's C7 Chromebook

The silver-finish Samsung Chromebook (that's it's full name, really) is priced at $249.99. Like the Acer, it offers an 11.6" high-definition display, 2GB memory, Wi-Fi connectivity, and a built-in webcam (standard definition instead of the Acer's high def). Instead of a hard disk, you get 16GB of faster solid state storage. The Samsung is a little smaller than the Acer, at 0.69" high compared to 1.1" for the Acer; it's also more than a half pound lighter, at just 2.4 pounds. Battery life is also better—6.5 hours for the Samsung, versus 4 hours for the Acer.

The Samsung Chromebook

3G Chromebook

Samsung's Chromebook is also available in a model with both Wi-Fi and 3G wireless connectivity—which means you can connect it to your cellular data network when there are no Wi-Fi hotspots around. The 3G version sells for $329.99.

HP is a newer entrant into the Chromebook market, with its Pavilion Chromebook (model 14-c010us). HP's Chromebook is unique in having a larger 14" screen, which is nice for viewing but limits battery life to just over 4 hours. Other than the screen, specs are similar to the Samsung Chromebook—2GB memory, 16GB solid state storage, and such. Weight is a little heavier, at 3.96 pounds, and the price is also a little higher, at $329.99.

HP's 14" Pavilion Chromebook

The final current Chromebook manufacturer is Lenovo, which aims its Thinkpad X131e Chromebook squarely at the education market. The Thinkpad Chromebook looks more rugged than its competitors, and adds Lenovo's unique nub-like TrackPoint stick controller. In terms of specs, it offers an 11.6" screen, 4GB memory, 16GB solid state storage, and 6.5-hour battery life. The price is relatively high, at $429.99—but then again, Lenovo has no plans at present to sell this unit direct to consumers, only to K-12 educational institutions, which have unique needs.

Lenovo's Thinkpad Chromebook

The following table compares the third-generation Chromebooks.

Chromebook Model Comparison

	Acer C7	Samsung Chromebook	HP Pavilion Chromebook	Lenovo Thinkpad Chromebook
List price	$199.99	$249.99	$329.99	$429.99
Screen size	11.6"	11.6"	14"	11.6"
Resolution (pixels)	1366 × 768	1366 × 768	1366 × 768	1366 × 768
Dimensions	8.0" × 11.2" × 1.1"	8.1" × 11.4" × 0.69"	9.37" × 13.66" × 0.83"	N/A (1.3" thick)
Weight	3.04 lbs.	2.43 lbs.	3.96 lbs.	3.92 lbs.
Battery life	4 hours	6.5 hours	4 hours, 15 minutes	6.5 hours
Wi-Fi wireless connectivity	Yes (802.11 a/b/g/n)	Yes (802.11 a/b/g/n)	Yes (802.11 a/b/g/n)	Yes (802.11 a/b/g/n)
Memory	2GB	2GB	2GB	4GB
Solid state data storage	None	16GB	16GB	16GB
Hard drive storage	320GB	None	None	None
Processor	1.1GHz Dual-core Intel Celeron	1.7GHz Samsung Exynos 5 Dual	1.1GHz Dual-core Intel Celeron	Intel Celeron
USB ports	3 (USB 2.0)	2 (1 USB 2.0 + 1 USB 3.0)	3 (USB 2.0)	3 (1 USB 2.0 + 2 USB 3.0)

	Acer C7	Samsung Chromebook	HP Pavilion Chromebook	Lenovo Thinkpad Chromebook
Memory card slot	2-in-1 (SD/MMC)	3-in-1 (SD/SDHC/SDXC)	2-in-1 (SD/MMC)	N/A
External video port(s)	VGA, HDMI	HDMI	HDMI	VGA, HDMI
Ethernet port	Yes	No	Yes	Yes
Built-in webcam	Yes	Yes	Yes	Yes
Webcam resolution	HD	VGA	HD	HD
Operating system	Google Chrome OS	Google Chrome OS	Google Chrome OS	Google Chrome OS

Google Chromebook Pixel

There's one more Chromebook to consider, although it's definitely not aimed at the general consumer market. Google's new Chromebook Pixel features an ultra-high resolution display, bigger screen, and state-of-the-art hardware design—but sells for $1,299. Learn more in Appendix B, "Google Chromebook Pixel."

Samsung Chromebook 550

Some outlets still have available Samsung's second generation Chromebook 550. This model has a slightly larger 12.1" display, 4GB memory, an HD webcam, and 4-in-1 memory card slot. It weighs 3.3 pounds and promises 6 hours of battery life. The big downside is the cost—$449 for a Wi-Fi only model, or $549 for a model with both Wi-Fi and 3G wireless connectivity.

If you're in the market for a Chromebox for your living room, there's just one model to choose from. The Samsung Series 3 Chromebox is run by a 1.9GHz Intel Celeron B840 dual-core processor and includes 4GB memory and 16GB solid state storage. It's a compact device, measuring just 7.5" × 7.5" × 1.28". It comes with built-in 802.11 a/b/g/n Wi-Fi, six USB ports, and DisplayPort and DVI outputs. The Series 3 Chromebox sells for $329.99.

The Samsung Series 3 Chromebox

Samsung Chromebook

Unboxing and Setting Up Your New Chromebook

Setting up a new Windows or Mac computer can be a daunting process. There are all sorts of questions to answer and configurations to make. It's typically a process that takes a half hour or more, and no one likes doing it.

Setting up a new Chromebook is different. The unboxing and setup process typically takes less than 15 minutes, and there's really not much to it. Read on to learn what you need to do.

Unboxing Your Chromebook

A typical third-generation Chromebook is a simple affair. Even the box itself is simple, small and lightweight, and, believe it or not, easy to open.

What do you find when you open the box? Well, every manufacturer does it differently, but here's what Samsung packs inside its Chromebook box:

- The Chromebook itself, wrapped for protection

- AC adapter and power cable

- Instruction manual and quick start guide

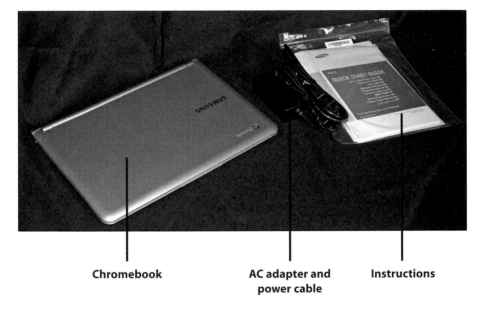

Chromebook   **AC adapter and**   **Instructions**
                       power cable

That's it. Obviously, there are no software or operating system disks because all of that is handled over the Internet. (And, as an added bonus, a Chromebook does not come with trial software versions or "crapware" pre-installed; you get a clean desktop on first boot up.)

Turning on Your Chromebook—For the Very First Time

Google claims that it takes less than a minute to set up a new Chromebook. The actual setup time is a bit longer than that, but only because the Chromebook goes online to download the latest version of the Chrome OS. That pushes the setup time to 10 to 15 minutes, depending on the speed of your Internet connection. Still, it's a relatively fast and painless process.

Charging the Battery

Out of the box, it's likely that your Chromebook's battery is not fully charged. For that reason, you need to plug it into an external power source during initial setup and then leave your Chromebook plugged in for several hours to charge the battery.

Setting Up a Chromebook

Before you use your new Chromebook, you need to unbox it, plug it in, and set it up.

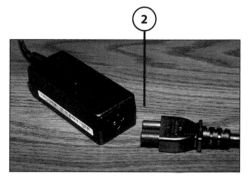

Google Account

Setup is easiest if you have a working Google Account before you start working with your new Chromebook. Although you can create a new Google Account during the setup process, it goes a lot faster if you can just enter your Google Account username and password. You can create a (free) Google Account from any web browser on any computer; just go to accounts.google.com/ NewAccount and follow the onscreen instructions.

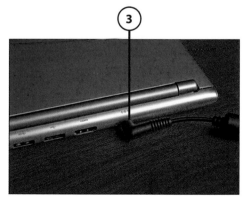

1. Remove the Chromebook from its box.

2. Connect the AC adapter to the power cable.

3. Connect the AC adapter to the power connector on the back of the Chromebook.

4. Plug the power cable into a work- ing power outlet.

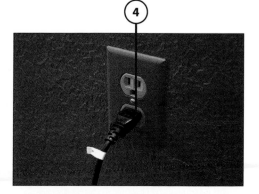

5. Open the Chromebook.

6. Press the Power button.

7. When the Welcome window appears, select your language from the list.

8. Select your keyboard from the list (typically US Keyboard).

9. Select your (wireless) network from the list.

Wireless Connections

Read more about managing Wi-Fi and 3G connections in Chapter 5, "Working Wirelessly."

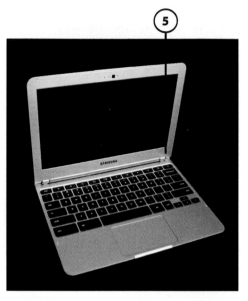

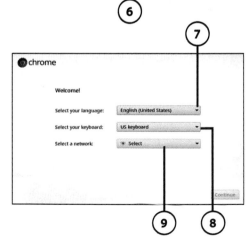

10. Enter your network password in the Join Wi-Fi Network window.

Secure Networks

Most home wireless networks are secure networks, which means you need to supply the appropriate password to access the network. In contrast, many public wireless networks are open networks, which means there is no password necessary to gain access.

11. Click the Connect button to return to the Welcome window.

12. Click the Continue button.

13. Read the Chrome OS Terms and then click the Accept and Continue button.

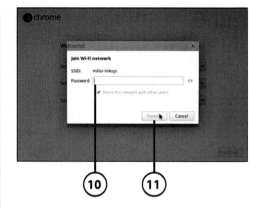

14. Chrome checks for operating system updates. This might take several minutes. When the update is complete, your Chromebook restarts. After restarting, your Chromebook displays the Sign In window.

15. If you already have a Google Account, enter your email address and password and then click the Sign in button. If you do not yet have a Google Account, click the Create a Google Account Now link and follow the onscreen instructions. To use your computer as a guest without signing in, click the Skip Sign-In and Browse as Guest link.

16. Choose a picture to display for your account on the sign-in screen and then click OK. Google Chrome launches and displays the Welcome to Your Chromebook window.

Change Your Picture

You can change your account picture at any later date. Find out how in Chapter 4, "Managing Multiple Users."

17. Click the options in the window to learn how to use your Chromebook's touchpad, save and access files, and use other Chrome OS functions.

18. Click the X at the top-right corner to close the window.

You only need to set up your Chromebook once. After you've completed this initial setup, you go directly to the login screen each time you start up.

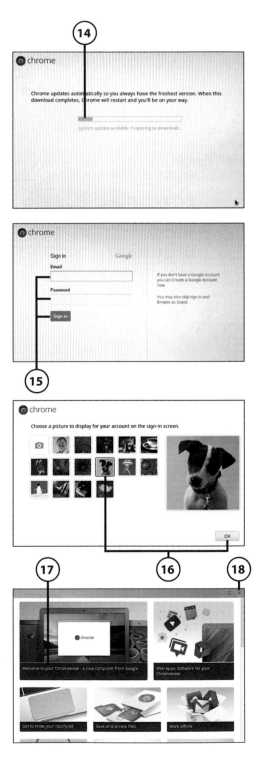

>>>Go Further

CONNECTING A CHROMEBOX

If you're the proud owner of a Chromebox, you not only have to deal with the initial setup (same as with a Chromebook), but also with connecting it to the necessary accessories to use it on your desktop. Fortunately, it's not that difficult.

We'll start with connecting the Chromebox to a monitor. The Samsung Chromebox comes with two different types of video connectors on the back of the unit. You have a DVI connector and two DisplayPort connectors; which connector you use depends on what type of connector you have on the back of your monitor. Use DVI for the best-quality connection; use DisplayPort (along with a DisplayPort-to-VGA cable) if your monitor only has a VGA connector.

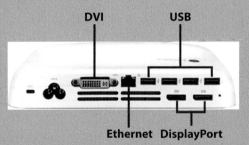

You also need to connect a keyboard and mouse to your Chromebox. Just connect each device to separate USB ports on the Chromebox. If you're using a wireless mouse or keyboard, connect the accompanying wireless mini-receiver to one of your Chromebox's USB ports.

Naturally, you also need to connect your Chromebox to your home network to connect to the Internet. The Chromebox has built-in Wi-Fi if you want to connect wirelessly, or you can connect via Ethernet using the Chromebox's back-panel Ethernet connector.

Creating a New Google Account

You must have a Google Account to use your Chromebook. Your Google Account serves as your user account in Chrome OS.

Guest Account

Although you can use a Chromebook with a guest account, this type of access has limited functionality. Read more about guest accounts in Chapter 4.

Creating a Google Account

A Google Account is completely free; it's necessary not just for using your Chromebook, but also for accessing any Google application, such as Gmail or Google Docs. It's easiest to create your Google Account before you first set up your Chromebook, although you can also create a new account during the Chromebook setup process.

1. Turn on your Chromebook, proceed to the sign-in screen, and click the Create a Google Account Now link. The Chrome browser connects to the Web and displays the Create a New Google Account page.

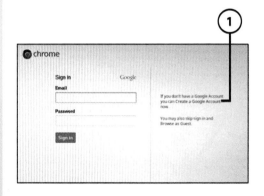

2. Enter your first and last name into the Name boxes.

3. Enter the name you'd like to use as a login into the Choose Your Username box.

Availability

If someone else is already using your chosen username, Google prompts you to try another name.

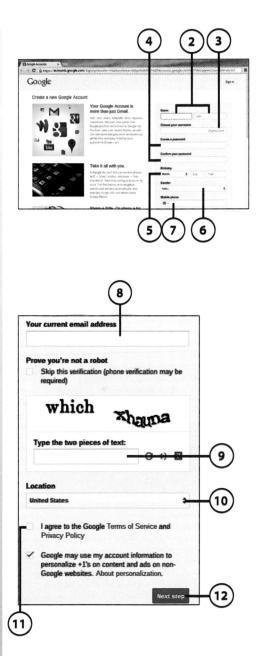

4. Enter your desired password (minimum of eight characters) into the Create a Password box and then re-enter it into the Confirm Your Password box.

5. Use the Birthday controls to enter the month, day, and year you were born.

6. Pull down the Gender list and select Female, Male, or Other.

7. Enter your mobile phone number into the Mobile Phone box.

8. Enter an existing email address into the Your Current Email Address box.

9. Enter the verification text into the Type the Two Pieces of Text box.

10. Pull down the Location list and select your current country.

11. Check to agree to Google's terms of service.

12. Click the Next Step button.

13. Add a profile photo if you want. (This is optional.) To add your photo, click the Add Profile Photo button and select the photo to use. Otherwise, click the Next Step button.

14. You've now created your account, and Google displays your new Gmail address. Click the Continue to Gmail button to set up your Gmail account, or close the window to proceed with the rest of your setup.

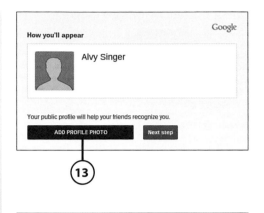

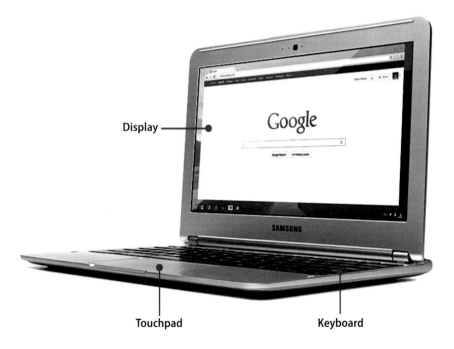

Display

Touchpad

Keyboard

In this chapter, you become familiar with the various pieces and parts of your new Chromebook, as well as how to use the keyboard and touchpad.

Getting to Know Your Chromebook

A Chromebook looks much like a traditional netbook or notebook computer. The lid opens to reveal the LCD display and keyboard, and there are ports and connectors and such along all sides of the case.

Before you use your Chromebook, you need to know what all these items are and what they do. You also want to get to know the Chromebook's keyboard and touchpad, which are a bit different from those found on other computers.

Getting to Know Your Chromebook

A Chromebook is like a simplified version of a traditional notebook computer. There are fewer ports and connectors, and also fewer keys on the keyboard and touchpad. That makes it easier to operate—if you know where everything is located.

As an example, we'll take a close look at features present on the best-selling model, the Samsung Chromebook. Other Chromebooks from Acer, HP, and Lenovo have similar features, as well as their own unique feature sets.

Not Included

Because a Chromebook is streamlined by design, it lacks some of the connections found in a traditional Windows or Mac computer. For example, there is no CD/DVD drive—which helps contribute to the Chromebook's light weight and small form factor.

Screen

When you open the Chromebook case, the screen is the first thing you see. Most Chromebooks have a screen 11.6" in diameter, with a widescreen aspect ratio. This is an LCD screen, typically backlit, for decent viewing even under bright light.

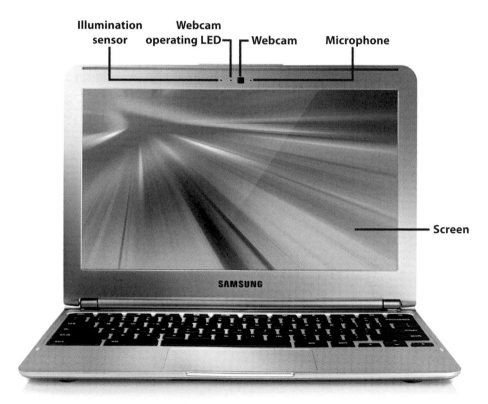

Illumination Sensor

Above the screen, grouped in the middle of the frame, are four key items. The first of these, on the left, is the illumination sensor. Your Chromebook uses this to sense the level of ambient light, and adjusts the screen brightness accordingly. If there's a lot of light, it increases the screen brightness; if there is less light, it decreases the screen brightness.

Webcam

All current Chromebooks come with a built-in camera, also known as a *webcam*. The webcam is located directly above the screen, in the middle of the frame. You can use the webcam to conduct video chats and conferences, make video calls, create recorded videos, and take still photographs of yourself.

When you're using the webcam, the webcam's operating LED lights. This LED is located directly to the left of the webcam, above the Chromebook's screen.

Microphone

The Chromebook's microphone is located above the screen on the middle right. It is used to capture audio during video chats, conferences, calls, and recordings. You can also use it for audio chats and Internet phone calls.

Keyboard

The keyboard is located on the base of the Chromebook. It's a little different from a traditional Windows or Mac keyboard in that nonessential keys have been removed and web-specific keys have been added. Learn more about the Chromebook's keyboard in the "Using the Keyboard" section, later in this chapter.

Touchpad

The Chromebook's touchpad is located directly below the primary keyboard. It functions as your Chromebook's mouse and cursor controller. Note that the touchpad does not include a right or left click button; instead, you tap the touchpad itself to click. Learn more in the "Using the Touchpad" section, later in this chapter.

Memory Card Slot

On the left side of the Chromebook, on the edge of the base section closest to the screen, is a 3-in-1 slot for inserting memory cards. You can insert SD, SDHC, and SDXC memory cards into this slot. You can use this slot to access photos from a digital camera, MP3 audio files, or even stored video files.

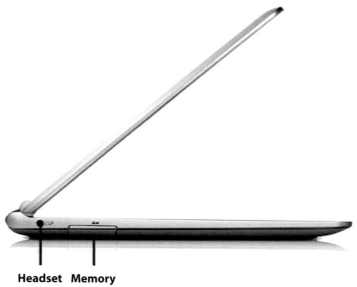

Headset   Memory
jack   card slot

Headset Jack

The left side of the case also features a headset jack, which you can use to connect headphones or earbuds for listening to your Chromebook's audio.

Acer C7

The Acer C7 Chromebook has similar ports to the Samsung Chromebook, but in different places. (All of the Acer's connectors are on the left and right side of the unit, not on the back.) The Acer also offers a VGA port to connect to an external computer monitor, and an Ethernet port to connect to wired home and business networks.

HP Pavilion Chromebook

HP's Pavilion Chromebook also has similar ports in different places. Most of the HP's connectors are on the right side of the case, including an Ethernet connector for wired networks.

USB Ports

There are no connectors on the right side of the Samsung Chromebook. Instead, the rest of the connectors are located on the back of the unit.

First up are two USB ports. The port on the left is compatible with the new USB 3.0 standard; the one on the right is a USB 2.0 port. You can use these ports to connect any USB devices to your Chromebook.

Power connector

Status indicator

HDMI connector

USIM card slot

USB 2.0 port

USB 3.0 port

USIM Cards

The 3G version of the Samsung Chromebook includes a slot for a USIM card. This covered slot is on the back of the unit, to the left of the USB ports.

HDMI Connector

To the right of the USB ports, on the back of the unit, is an HDMI connector. Use this connector to connect your Chromebook to a flat panel TV or audio/video receiver; it transmits both HD video and audio from your Chromebook.

Status Indicator

Next to the HDMI connector is a small LED light that serves as a status indicator for your Chromebook. The indicator glows green when the Chromebook is running on external power and the battery is fully charged; it glows red when running on external power and the battery is being charged, and it is off when the computer is running on battery power.

Power Connector

The final item on the back of the Chromebook, on the far right, is the DC jack. This is where you connect the AC adapter to your Chromebook for external power.

AC/DC

Your Chromebook natively runs on DC (direct current) power, such as that supplied by the internal battery. Because the electricity from a wall outlet is AC (alternating current), the external power adapter is necessary to convert the AC power to DC power.

Using the Keyboard

The Chromebook keyboard is a simplified version of a traditional keyboard. It's simplified in that several lesser-used keys are missing; this lets your Chromebook make the remaining keys bigger in a smaller space.

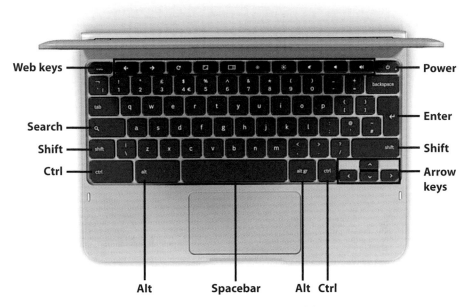

Web keys — Power

Search

Shift — Enter

Ctrl — Shift

— Arrow keys

Alt   Spacebar   Alt Ctrl

The first keys that are missing are the traditional function (F1, F2, F3, and so on) keys normally found on the top row of the keyboard. In place of these functions keys, your Chromebook features a row of "web keys" that perform specific functions for web browsing. The following table describes these web keys found on the top row of the Chromebook keyboard.

Web Key	Function
←	Go to the previous page in your browser history.
→	Go to the next page in your browser history.
⟳	Reload the current page.
⬘	Open the current page in full-screen mode.
▢▢	Switch to next window.
☼	Decrease screen brightness.
☀	Increase screen brightness.
🔇	Mute/unmute the audio.
🔉	Decrease the volume.
🔊	Increase the volume.

The row of web keys also includes your Chromebook's Power button, which you use to turn your Chromebook on or off. The LED on this button shows your Chromebook's operating status: It lights on when your Chromebook is running, blinks when your Chromebook is in sleep mode, and is dark when your Chromebook is turned completely off. There's also an Esc key on the far left side of this row.

Beneath the top row of web keys is the expected row of numeric (1, 2, 3, and so on) keys. This row also includes the backspace key, which deletes the previous character entered.

The next four rows contain the traditional alphabetic (a, b, c, and so on) keys. At the ends of these rows are your Chromebook's Shift, Ctrl, Alt, and Enter keys, along with a grouping of four arrow keys for navigation.

Note that there is no Caps Lock key on the Chromebook; if you need to type successive capital letters, you need to hold down the Shift key as necessary.

 Where you might expect to find a Caps Lock key is a new Chrome-specific Search key. Press this key to go to the address bar on the New Tab page to initiate a web search.

It's Not All Good

If you're used to a traditional Windows or Mac computer, you'll find several keys missing from the Chromebook keyboard. Here are the keys you're used to that aren't on the Chromebook:

- F1–F12 function keys
- Caps Lock
- Insert
- Delete
- Home
- End
- Page Down
- Page Up
- Windows
- Menu

Turn the Search Key into a Caps Lock Key

You can, with a little work, turn Chrome's Search key into a Caps Lock key. Click your profile picture at the bottom right of the screen and select Settings. When the Settings page appears, go to the Device section and click the Keyboard Settings button. When the Keyboard Settings dialog box appears, pull down the Search list and select Caps Lock. Click the OK button when done.

Using the Touchpad

Just below the keyboard is your Chromebook's touchpad, which provides the same functionality as an external mouse. That is, you use the touchpad to move the onscreen cursor and click and select items onscreen.

Touchpad

External Mouse

If you don't like the touchpad, you can connect an external mouse to one of the Chromebook's USB ports. See the "Connecting External Devices" section, later in this chapter, to learn how.

Moving the Cursor

You use your finger on the touchpad to move the cursor around the Chromebook screen.

1. Place your finger lightly on the touchpad.

2. Move your finger in the direction in which you want to move the cursor.

The mouse cursor moves in the direction you moved your finger.

Clicking the Cursor

You can either single-click or double-click items on your Chromebook's screen. Single-clicking is most common.

1. Move the cursor on top of the item to click.
2. Tap your finger anywhere on the touchpad.

To double-click an item, tap twice instead of once.

Right-Clicking the Cursor

Many useful functions often appear via a pop-up menu when you right-click an item onscreen. But how do you right-click a touchpad that doesn't have a right button?

1. Move the cursor to the item you want to right-click.
2. Place two fingers anywhere on the touchpad and press once.

Dragging an Item

To move an item to another position on screen, you drag it to a new position.

1. Move the cursor to the item you want to move.
2. Press and hold the touchpad while you drag the item to a new location.
3. Lift your finger from the touchpad to "drop" the item in place.

Scrolling the Screen

If you're viewing a long web page or editing a long document, you need to scroll down the screen to see the entire page. Although you can do this with the keyboard's up arrow and down arrow keys, you can also scroll with the touchpad.

1. Place two fingers lightly on the touchpad, but do *not* press down on the touchpad.
2. Drag your fingers down to scroll down the page.
3. Drag your fingers up to scroll up the page.

PAGE SCROLLING

On a traditional notebook PC, you can scroll up or down one page at a time by using the Page Up and Page Down keys. Unfortunately, there are no Page Up and Page Down keys on a Chromebook keyboard, so that option is not available. You can, however, press the Alt+Up Arrow and Alt+Down Arrow key combinations to scroll up or down one page at a time. You can also press the Spacebar to scroll down a page.

Adjusting Touchpad Sensitivity

If you find that your touchpad is too sensitive, or not sensitive enough, you can adjust the sensitivity of the touchpad.

1. Click your profile picture at the bottom of the screen to display the pop-up menu.

2. Select Settings.

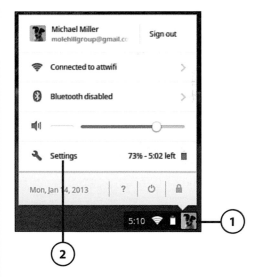

3. When the Settings page appears, select the Settings tab, on the left.

4. Go to the Device section and drag the Touchpad Speed slider to the left to make it less sensitive, or to the right to make it more sensitive.

③

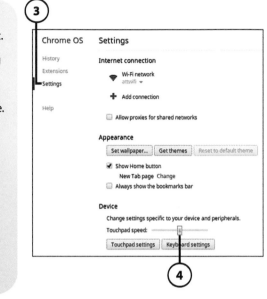

Tap-to-Click

By default, you tap within the touch area of the touchpad to click an onscreen item. If you'd prefer to press in the touch area instead, check the Touchpad Settings button and then uncheck the Enable Tap-to-Click box. Click OK when done.

④

Connecting External Devices

Although a Chromebook is a relatively self-contained unit, you can connect various external devices to the machine, typically via USB.

Connecting an External Mouse

If you don't like your Chromebook's built-in touchpad, you can connect an external mouse to one of the USB ports. You can connect either a corded or cordless model.

①

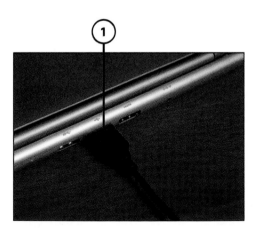

1. Connect the cable from the external mouse to one of the Chromebook's USB ports. (If you're connecting a wireless mouse, plug the wireless receiver into the USB port.)

2. Your Chromebook should immediately recognize the external mouse and make it available for use.

Connecting an External Keyboard

You can also connect a larger external keyboard to your Chromebook via USB. As with an external mouse, you can connect either a corded or cordless keyboard.

1. Connect the cable from the external keyboard to one of the Chromebook's USB ports. (If you're connecting a wireless keyboard, plug the wireless receiver into the USB port.)

2. Your Chromebook should immediately recognize the external keyboard and make it available for use.

Connecting to a Large-Screen TV

If you're watching streaming movies or television programs, the 11.6" Chromebook screen doesn't quite deliver a big-screen viewing experience. Fortunately, you can use your Chromebook to deliver streaming Internet programming to your living room TV—and watch it all on the big screen.

1. Connect one end of an HDMI cable to the HDMI connector on your Chromebook.

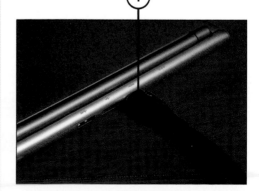

2. Connect the other end of the HDMI cable to an HDMI input on your television set or audio/video receiver.

3. Switch your TV or receiver to the proper HDMI input.

   You should now see on your television screen whatever is playing on your Chromebook.

External Storage

You can also connect certain external storage devices to your Chromebook via USB. Learn more in Chapter 7, "Managing Files and Using External Storage."

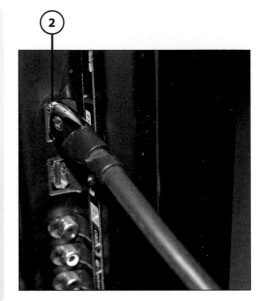

Adjusting Brightness and Volume

Your Chromebook includes dedicated keys, located in the top row of the keyboard, for adjusting screen brightness and audio volume.

Adjusting Screen Brightness

You can make your Chromebook display brighter or darker. A brighter display might look nicer, especially under bright lighting, but can drain the battery faster. Dimming the screen a tad can still look good while maximizing battery life.

1. To increase screen brightness, press the Increase Brightness key.

2. To decrease screen brightness, press the Decrease Brightness key.

   One press of either key changes the brightness by one level.

>>>Go Further

CLEANING THE SCREEN

It's important to keep your Chromebook's LCD screen clean. You should clean the screen with a soft cloth that's slightly dampened with a special computer cleansing fluid. You can find this fluid at any consumer electronics or computer supply store. Squirt the fluid directly on your cleaning cloth, and then lightly wipe the screen in a single direction; using too much force can damage the screen.

Adjusting and Muting the Volume

Whether you're using your Chromebook's built-in speaker or listening through headphones or earbuds, you'll probably need to adjust the volume level at some point.

1. To increase the volume level, press the Increase Volume key.

2. To decrease the volume level, press the Decrease Volume key.

3. To mute the volume, press the Mute button; press the button again to unmute the sound.

Apps panel   Desktop

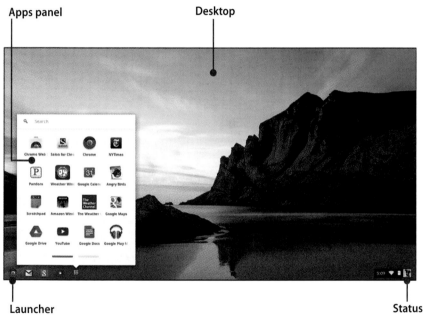

Launcher   Status
                                            area

In this chapter, you find out how to turn your Chromebook on and off, and how to navigate the Chrome desktop.

Using Chrome OS and the Chrome Desktop

Using a Chromebook is similar to using a traditional notebook computer, but faster. Because there's less operating system overhead involved, as well as fewer internal components, a Chromebook boots up much quicker than a Windows or Mac machine; it wakes up from sleep mode almost immediately.

What you find after you start up your Chromebook, however, might not be totally familiar to you, especially if you're used to using a Windows or Mac notebook. To use your Chromebook, you need to get used to the Chrome OS interface.

Starting Up and Shutting Down

The most basic computer operations are turning the computer on and turning it off. Your Chromebook should start up in 10 seconds or so, and power down almost immediately.

Starting Up and Logging In

Your Chromebook can be run either on battery power or connected to an external AC power source. After it powers up, you then have to log into the computer with your username and password.

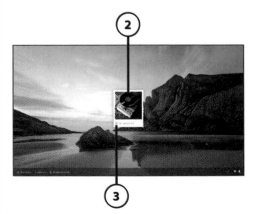

1. To power up your Chromebook, simply open the case and lift the LCD display panel.

   Or

1. If the LCD panel is already opened, press the Power button.

Power Button

The small LCD on the Power button lights when your Chromebook is turned on.

2. When the login screen appears, select your user account (if you have more than one account on this machine).

3. Enter your password.

4. Press Enter.

   Google Chrome now launches and displays the desktop.

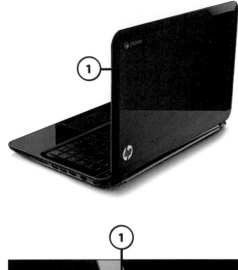

Putting Your Chromebook to Sleep

Although you can completely power off your Chromebook, you might prefer to enter sleep mode instead. This is good for when you're not actively using the Chromebook for a period of time, but expect to resume use soon; it conserves your Chromebook's battery life.

The advantage of sleep mode over powering down your Chromebook is that when you're ready to resume use, your Chromebook resumes operation immediately. If you instead opt to power down and then restart your Chromebook, you have to sit through the (admittedly short) startup process and then reenter your password.

Screensaver

Your Chromebook automatically turns off its screen after 6 minutes of inactivity (8 minutes if you're using external power). You redisplay the screen by swiping across the touchpad or pressing any key on the keyboard.

1. To enter sleep mode, close the lid of your Chromebook.
2. To wake up from sleep mode, open the lid of your Chromebook.

Powering Off Your Chromebook

Shutting off your Chromebook is a simple matter of pressing the Power key. Unlike other operating systems, Chrome OS does not require a menu operation to power off.

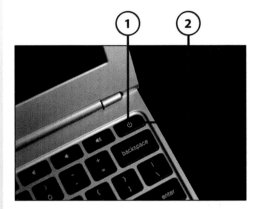

1. Press and hold the Power button for 2 seconds. The screen shrinks and, if you release the button now, Chrome goes into screen lock mode.

2. Continue holding the Power button for an additional 2 seconds.

   Your Chromebook now completely powers off. You can restart your Chromebook by following the startup procedure previously described.

Locking the Screen

Chrome OS features a screen lock mode that displays the Chrome login screen. To access screen lock mode, press and hold the Power button for 2 seconds and then release the Power button. To resume normal operation, select your username, enter your password, and press Enter. To power off from screen lock mode, simply close the Chromebook's lid.

It's Not All Good

Forcing a Shutdown

If for some reason your Chromebook freezes or refuses to shut down normally, you can force a shutdown by pressing and holding the Power button for at least 8 seconds.

Navigating the Chrome OS Desktop

The latest version of Chrome OS features a desktop interface that looks and feels similar to the Windows or Mac OS desktop. You can open multiple windows to appear on the desktop, and size and arrange those windows as you like.

Desktop

Launcher   **Status area**

>>>Go Further

AUTOHIDE THE LAUNCHER

By default, the Launcher and status area always appear at the bottom of the desktop screen. If you want a little more screen room, you can configure the Launcher/status area to automatically hide until you move your cursor to the bottom of the screen.

To autohide the Launcher and status area, right-click at the bottom of the screen and then check Autohide Launcher. To deactivate the autohide feature, right-click the bottom of the screen and uncheck Autohide Launcher.

Launcher

At the bottom left of the desktop is the Launcher. This area contains icons for your most popular applications. By default, the Launcher hosts icons for New Tab (in a Chrome browser window), Gmail, Google Search, YouTube, and Apps; you can also pin other apps to the Launcher. Click an icon to launch that app in a new window.

The right-most icon in the Launcher is labeled Apps. When you click the Apps icon, Chrome displays the Apps List panel. The Apps List includes all the apps you've installed or used on your Chromebook, as well as those pre-installed by Google and the Chromebook's manufacturer. You can add more apps to the Apps List by visiting the Chrome Web Store.

___

Chrome Web Store
Learn more about Chrome apps and the Chrome Web Store in Chapter 11, "Using Chrome Apps and Extensions."

___

You can also search your apps and favorite websites from the Apps List panel. Just enter your query into the Search box at the top and then press Enter. Chrome displays a list of matching apps and web pages.

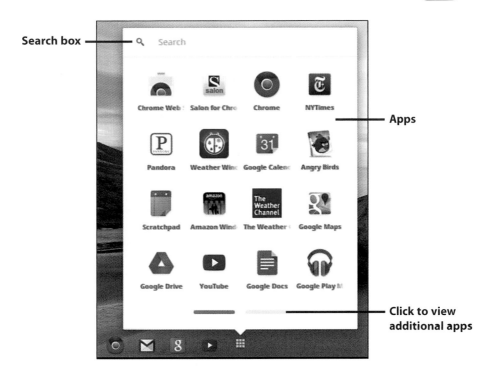

Status Area

At the bottom right of the Chrome desktop is the status area. This area includes information about your system and access to your personal settings.

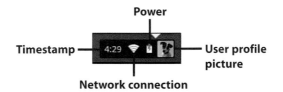

There are three main status icons in the status area: Timestamp, Network Connection, and Power. A fourth icon displays the profile picture for the currently signed-in user.

The following table details the icons you might encounter in the status area.

Chrome OS Status Icons

Icon	Status Type	Description
4:28	Timestamp	Displays current time.
	Network Connection	Connected to a non-secure Wi-Fi network. The number of "lit" signal bars indicates the strength of your connection.
	Network Connection	Connected to a secure Wi-Fi network.
	Network Connection	No Wi-Fi connection.
	Network Connection	Connected to a wired network.
	Network Connection	Connected to a wired network; no network connection.
	Network Connection	Connected to a mobile 3G network (3G Chromebooks only). The number of "lit" signal bars indicates the strength of your connection.
	Network Connection	Connecting to a mobile 3G network (3G Chromebooks only).
	Network Connection	If you're using Verizon's 3G network, you've run out of available mobile data on your plan (3G Chromebooks only). You need to purchase more data to continue using the mobile network.
	Power	Operating on battery power. The amount of battery time left is indicated by the "fill" level of the battery icon.
	Power	Operating on external power, recharging battery.

Click anywhere in the status area to display the Status panel. You can do the following from this panel:

- Sign out of the current account or switch to another account by clicking Sign Out.

- Change your network connection by clicking Connected To.

- Activate external Bluetooth devices by clicking Bluetooth.

- Raise or lower your Chromebook's volume level by using the speaker control.

- Configure additional Chrome OS settings by clicking Settings.

- View how much battery power you have left on the current charge.

- Display Chrome's help system by clicking the question mark (?) icon.

- Move your Chromebook into sleep mode by clicking the power icon.

- Lock your system (requires your password to resume normal operation) by clicking the lock icon.

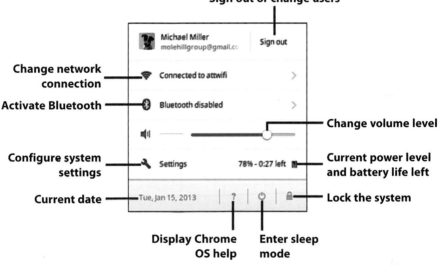

Sign out or change users

Michael Miller
molehillgroup@gmail.co   Sign out

Change network connection — Connected to attwifi

Activate Bluetooth — Bluetooth disabled

Change volume level

Configure system settings — Settings   78% - 0:27 left — **Current power level and battery life left**

Current date — Tue, Jan 15, 2013   ? ⏻ 🔒 — **Lock the system**

Display Chrome OS help   **Enter sleep mode**

Chrome OS Settings

Learn more about configuring Chrome's settings in Chapter 6, "Configuring and Personalizing Chrome OS."

Navigating Windows and Tabs

Every app you open in Chrome appears in a Chrome browser window. This window is much like the Chrome web browser available for both the Windows and Mac operating systems. Different apps appear in different tabs within the main window; you can also remove tabs from the browser to create multiple browser windows on the desktop.

View previous page
View next page
Reload current page
Display home page
Omnibox   **Tab**

Click to open
new tab

Customize and
Control button
Close window
Maximize window

Along the top of the Chrome browser are all your open tabs, as well as a small blank tab, that you use to open additional tabs. Below the row of tabs and indicators is Chrome's Omnibox. This is where you enter web page URLs or search queries. To the left of the Omnibox are buttons to switch to the previous and next pages viewed, and a Reload button for refreshing the current page.

To the right of the Address box is the Bookmark icon where you can bookmark pages to come back to later. Next to that is the Customize and Control Google Chrome button; click this button to display a menu of system settings for the Chrome browser and your Google Account.

When you open a new tab, Chrome displays its default home page. This New Tab tab displays those web pages you've most recently visited. There are links at the bottom of the page to view web pages viewed on other devices attached to your Google Account, recently closed tabs, and the Google Chrome Web Store.

Opening a New Chrome Window

If no window is currently open, you can open a new window by clicking the New Tab icon on the Launcher.

If a window is currently open, there are two ways to open a new window:

1. Click the Customize and Control button and then click New Window.

2. Press Ctrl+N from the Chromebook keyboard.

New Window from Tab

You can drag any existing tab from the browser window to the Chrome desktop. This opens a new window for the page or app in that tab.

Opening New Tabs

There are four ways to open a new tab in the current browser window:

1. Click the Customize and Control button and then click New tab.

2. Click the small blank tab at the end of the browser's tab row.

3. Click the New Tab icon on the Launcher.

4. Press Ctrl+T on the Chromebook keyboard.

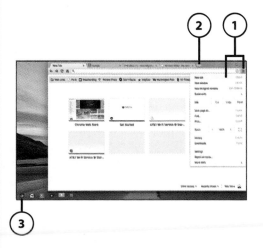

Navigating Tabs

Chrome can display multiple tabs, each displaying a different web page or running a specific web app.

1. Click a tab to go directly to that open tab.

2. Click the X on a tab to close it.

3. Press Ctrl+Tab to switch to the next open tab.

Managing Window Size

It's easy to change the size of any open window on the desktop.

1. Click the Maximize button on the top-right corner of the window to make the window full screen. Alternatively, press the Full Screen button on the Chromebook keyboard.

2. Click the Maximize button again to return a maximized window to its normal size.

3. Mouse over the Maximize button and select the middle icon to minimize a window to the Launcher. Alternatively, you can also drag the window to the Launcher.

4. Mouse over the Maximize button and select the left icon to dock a window to the left side of the screen. Alternatively, you can also drag the window to the left side of the screen.

5. Mouse over the Maximize button and select the right icon to dock a window to the right side of the screen. Alternatively, you can also drag the window to the right side of the screen.

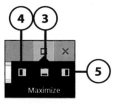

Maximize

6. To resize a window, mouse over any window edge or corner until the cursor changes shape and then drag the cursor to resize the window.

Switching Between Windows

Chrome enables you to open multiple windows, each with its own set of tabs, and then switch between windows. There are two ways to switch to the next open window in Chrome.

1. Press the Next Window button on the top row of your Chromebook's keyboard.

2. Press Alt+Tab on the Chromebook keyboard.

Switching Tabs

To switch between tabs in an open browser window, press Ctrl+Tab.

Closing the Window

Closing any open window is a one-click operation.

1. Click the X at the top right of the window.

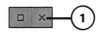

Add new
user to this
Chromebook

Browse the Web
via Guest account

Enter account
password

In this chapter, you find out how to create multiple users for your Chromebook, how to switch from user to user, and how to use Chromebook's Guest account

Managing Multiple Users

A Chromebook is only a piece of hardware; all your personal settings, information, and data are stored on the Web. As such, you can log into any Chromebook machine with your Google Account, and it will look and feel just like your own Chromebook. And it's easy enough for other users to log into your Chromebook, as well, and make it their own.

How easy is it to add new users to a Chromebook? Pretty easy, as you'll soon discover.

Adding Users to Your Chromebook

When you first started up your Chromebook, you were prompted to enter your Google Account name and password. This account becomes your default user account on your Chromebook. You can, however, add other users to your Chromebook—that is, let other people with Google Accounts use this particular Chromebook.

Add a User

You can let any number of users log onto your Chromebook, as long as they all have Google Accounts.

1. Click anywhere in the status area to display the Settings panel.

2. Click Sign Out.

3. From the login screen, click + Add User. The Sign In screen displays.

4. Enter the new user's Gmail address into the Email field.

5. Enter the user's Gmail password into the Password field.

6. Click the Sign In button.

7. Select a picture for the new account and then click the OK button.

Chrome displays the Welcome to Your Chromebook window. Close this window to begin using Chrome as normal. The next time you open your Chromebook, this account will be one of the options on the login screen.

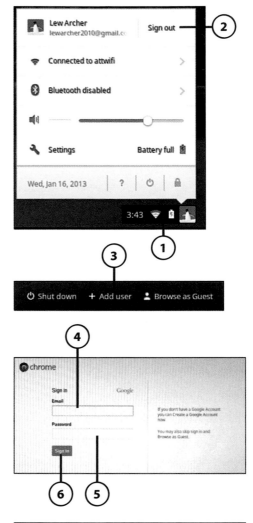

USING OTHER CHROMEBOOKS

With the Chrome OS, you're not limited to a single Chromebook. You can also use other people's Chromebooks, by logging into your Google Account on that machine.

When you log into any Chromebook with your Google Account, that Chromebook displays all the apps and personalization that you've made to your own Chromebook. In essence, your Chromebook settings travel from machine to machine; they're tied to your account in the cloud, not to any particular piece of hardware.

Editing User Information

Don't like the picture you've chosen for your Chromebook user account? It's easy enough to change—along with other information in your Google Account.

Change Your Profile Picture

Google Chrome lets you choose from a selection of built-in icons for your user account picture, upload an existing picture, or shoot a new picture using your webcam.

1. Click anywhere in the status area to display the Settings panel.

2. Click Settings to open the Settings page.

3. Scroll to the Users section and click the thumbnail image. The Change Picture panel displays. Use step 4, 5, or 6 as appropriate.

4. To use one of the built-in icons, click the image you want to use for your picture and then click OK.

5. To take a picture with your Chromebook's webcam and use it for your account picture, click the Camera icon. When the live image from your webcam appears, smile into the camera and click the green camera button. If you like the picture that results, click the OK button. (If you don't like what you see, click the Trash icon and take another picture.)

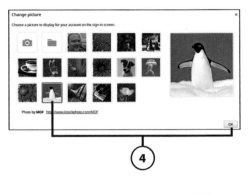

6. To upload a stored picture for your account picture, click the Folder icon. When the Select a File to Open panel appears, navigate to and select the file you want to upload and then click the Open button.

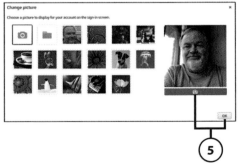

Edit Your Profile

Your Chromebook account is tied to your Google Account, in that they both use the same username (email address) and password. As a result, you can log into your account from any Chromebook.

Your Google Account is used by all Google services and applications, and includes your personal account profile. If this is a new Google Account, you need to create a new profile. You can also edit your profile at any time.

1. Open a new Chrome window and go to www.google.com.

2. Click your account name or picture in the top-right corner of the page and select View Profile. Your profile page displays.

3. Click the Edit Profile button. This makes everything in your profile editable.

4. Click the section of your profile you want to edit; this opens a panel for editing.

5. Enter the appropriate information for that section.

6. Click the Save button when you're done entering information for that section.

7. Move to the next section you want to edit and repeat steps 4 through 6. When you're done editing your profile, click the Done Editing button at the top of the page.

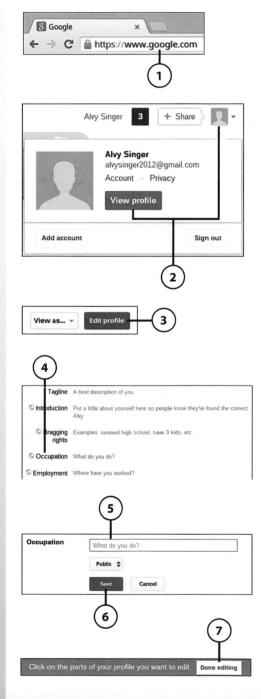

Google Account

A single Google Account provides your own personal access to all of Google's various sites and services. That includes personalized search results from Google's search engine (www.google.com), email service from Gmail (mail.google.com), online calendars on Google Calendar (www.google.com/calendar/), and your own account on Google+ (plus.google.com), Google's social network.

Switching Users

If you've created multiple user accounts for your Chromebook, it's easy to switch from one user account to another—without shutting down your machine.

Switch User Accounts

To switch users, you need to sign out from one account on your Chromebook and sign into another.

1. Click anywhere in the status area to display the Settings panel.

2. Click Sign Out.

3. Your Chromebook displays the login screen. Select the user account to log into, enter the password, and press Enter.

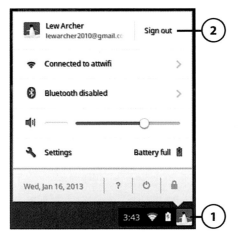

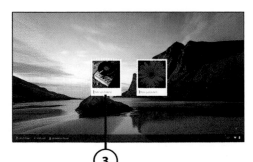

Log in as a Guest User

Any person can log into your Chromebook as a Guest user. A Guest user has limited use of the Chromebook; he or she can browse the Web, but not save or access files on your machine. In addition, a Guest user's browsing and search history are not saved.

1. Click anywhere in the status area to display the Settings panel.

2. Click Sign Out.

3. Your Chromebook now displays the log in screen. Click Browse as Guest.

Available wireless
networks

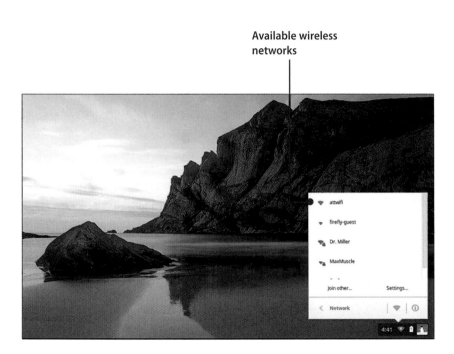

In this chapter, you find out how to connect to and manage wireless networks for your Chromebook.

→ Connecting to a Wi-Fi Network

→ Connecting to an Ethernet Network

→ Managing Network Connections

Working Wirelessly

Chrome OS is a web-based operating system; to fully use your Chromebook, you must be connected to the Internet. All Chromebooks include built-in Wi-Fi wireless connectivity, so you can connect to the Internet over any nearby Wi-Fi network.

Some Chromebooks also include 3G capability, so you can connect via a mobile data service when no Wi-Fi is available. And, despite the Chromebook being primarily a portable device, it's also possible to connect a Chromebook to a wired network to access the Internet. Which option you use depends on your own specific circumstances.

Connecting to a Wi-Fi Network

Most users will connect their Chromebooks to the Internet via some sort of Wi-Fi wireless connection. Wi-Fi is Chrome's default connection method, as most homes and offices are set up with Wi-Fi connectivity; there are also numerous public Wi-Fi hotspots available at coffee houses, hotels, restaurants, and the like.

Supported Networks

The current generation of Chromebooks can connect to 802.11 a/b/g/n Wi-Fi networks, using any of the following wireless security schemes: WEP, WPA-PSK, and WPA-Enterprise. At present, Chrome OS does not support networks that require security certificates.

Viewing Network Status

The Network icon in the status area at the bottom right of the Chrome desktop indicates the status of your Wi-Fi connection, as detailed in the following table.

Wi-Fi Status Icons

Icon	Status
▼	Connected to a Wi-Fi network
▼	No Wi-Fi connection

Enabling Wi-Fi on Your Chromebook

Wi-Fi connectivity is enabled by default on most Chromebooks. If necessary, however, you can enable Wi-Fi manually.

1. Click anywhere in the status area to display the Settings panel.

2. Click No Network; the settings panel changes.

3. Click Turn WiFi on.

Disabling Wi-Fi

If Wi-Fi is enabled, you can disable Wi-Fi by opening the Settings panel and clicking the Wi-Fi icon.

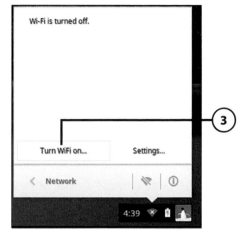

Connecting to an Open Wi-Fi Network

When Wi-Fi is enabled on your Chromebook, connecting to a Wi-Fi network is as easy as selecting the network from a list. Many Wi-Fi networks, especially public ones, are "open," meaning that anyone can connect without supplying a password.

1. Click anywhere in the status area to display the Status panel.

2. Click No Network.

3. Chrome displays a list of nearby available wireless networks. Open networks are marked with a regular wireless icon; private networks (those that require passwords to access) have a lock next to the icon. Click the open network to which you want to connect.

   The network name displays with the word "Connecting" next to it. When "Connecting" disappears, you're connected.

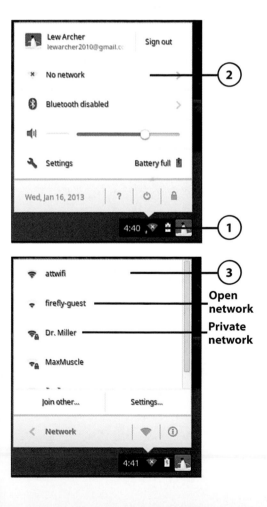

Open network

Private network

>>>Go Further

PUBLIC NETWORKS

Some public Wi-Fi networks, such as those you find in a coffee shop or hotel, might require additional log-in information after you've connected to the network. In most instances, a proprietary log-in screen appears when you first attempt to view a website; you then need to follow the onscreen instructions to connect.

For example, when you connect to Starbucks' Wi-Fi, you first connect to the open ATTWIFI network. When you enter the first URL into Chrome's Omnibox, you see the Starbucks log-in page. You must check the box indicating you accept the terms and conditions and then click a button to complete the connection.

In other instances, such as at some hotels, you might be asked to provide a password provided by the establishment when you first use your web browser. If the Wi-Fi service isn't free, you might also be asked to provide a credit card for billing, or okay billing to your room number.

Connecting to a Secure Wi-Fi Network

Many Wi-Fi networks, especially home and business networks, are secure, meaning they require a password for access. You need to supply this password to connect to a secure network.

1. Click anywhere in the status area to display the Status panel.

2. Click No Network.

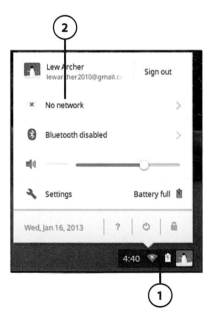

3. Chrome displays a list of nearby available wireless networks. Secure networks (those that require a password for access) are marked with a "locked" icon. Click the network to which you want to connect.

4. Enter the password for the network in the Join Wi-Fi Network dialog box and then click the Connect button.

Connecting to an Ethernet Network

In some instances, you get better performance by making a wired connection to your network instead of a wireless one. An Ethernet connection is both faster and more stable than a Wi-Fi connection; it's also more secure because it's virtually immune to outside hacking.

Because the Chromebook is designed to be a wireless device, however, connecting via Ethernet is a secondary option. In fact, the most popular model (the Samsung Chromebook) doesn't even have an Ethernet port. That doesn't mean that you can't connect a Samsung Chromebook via Ethernet; you just have to know how.

Connecting via Ethernet

If you have an Acer, HP, or Lenovo Chromebook, connecting to your network via Ethernet is as easy as connecting a cable.

1. Connect one end of an Ethernet cable to an Ethernet port on your Chromebook.

2. Connect the other end of the Ethernet cable into your network router.

The Network icon in the status area changes to an Ethernet icon and indicates the status of your connection.

It's Not All Good

No Access

An X on the Ethernet icon indicates that you're physically connected to the network but do not have network access.

Connecting via Ethernet (Samsung Chromebook)

To connect a Samsung Chromebook to a network via Ethernet, you need to purchase a USB Ethernet adapter. This low-cost adapter lets you connect an Ethernet cable to your Chromebook, via an open USB port.

1. Plug the USB Ethernet adapter into one of your Chromebook's USB ports.

2. Connect one end of an Ethernet cable to the adapter.

3. Connect the other end of the Ethernet cable into your network router.

The Network icon changes to an Ethernet icon and indicates the status of your connection.

NO NETWORKING

The Chromebook is designed as an Internet device; it is not a networking computer. Even though you connect to the Internet via a wireless network, you can't access other assets on the network.

This means that you can't use your Chromebook to access other computers connected to the network, or access files stored on the network. For that matter, other network computers can't see or access your Chromebook, even when it's connected through a given network.

For that matter, you can't use your Chromebook to connect to a virtual private network (VPN), such as those available in many large organizations. (Although VPN capability is being beta tested by Google, it's not yet activated.) All of this makes the Chromebook somewhat less useful as a corporate computing device.

The only way to share files with other network users is to access those files via a cloud-based services, such as Google Drive, or email the files using Gmail.

Managing Network Connections

If you connect to the Internet in different locations, chances are you connect through a variety of different wireless networks. Managing your available wireless networks, then, is important.

Automatically Connecting to a Network

If you have a favorite wireless network at a given location where multiple networks may be available, you can configure your Chromebook to automatically connect to your network of choice.

1. Make sure you're connected to the network in question and then click anywhere in the status area to display the Settings panel.

2. Click Connected To. The panel changes.

3. Click the currently connected network to display a panel for the currently connected network.

4. Check the Automatically Connect to This Network option.

5. Click the Close button.

Forgetting a Network

Chrome automatically saves details about each and every network you connect to. If there is a network to which it's unlikely you'll ever connect again, you can clear the details for that network—in effect, you're telling Chrome to forget that network.

1. Click anywhere in the status area to display the Settings panel.

2. Click Settings. The Settings page displays.

3. Go to the Internet Connection section, click the Wi-Fi Network menu, and select Preferred Networks.

4. Click the X next to the network you want to forget.

5. Click OK.

Viewing Network Details

In some circumstances, you might be asked to provide information about the wireless network to which you're connected. Chrome OS can display those details.

1. Make sure you're connected to the network in question and then click anywhere in the status area to display the Settings panel.

2. Click Connected To. The panel changes.

3. Click the currently connected network to display a panel for the network.

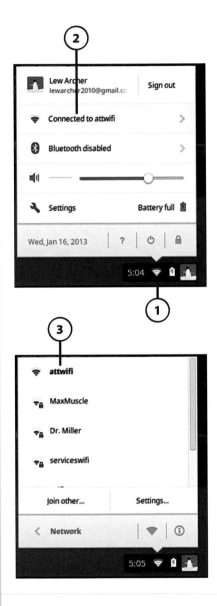

4. Click the Connection tab to see all information about this network.

④

attwifi
Connected | Wi-Fi network

Connection   Proxy

☑ Automatically connect to this network

Connection status:	Online state
SSID:	attwifi
BSSID:	00:1e:13:42:c2:10
IP address:	192.168.5.242
Subnet mask:	255.255.255.0
Gateway:	192.168.5.1
DNS server:	192.168.5.1
Frequency:	2412 MHz
Signal Strength:	59%
Hardware address:	20:02:AF:F5:6F:64

This network is shared with other users.

Disconnect   Close

Desktop
backgrounds

Types of
backgrounds

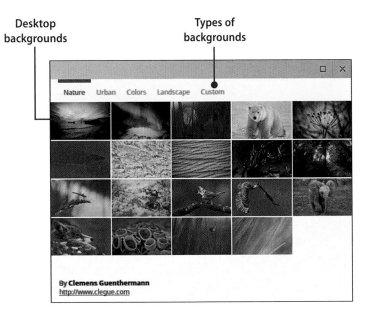

In this chapter, you discover the many configuration options available with Chrome OS, from changing Chrome's startup behavior to selecting a new desktop background.

→ Personalizing the Desktop
→ Configuring the Chrome Browser
→ Configuring Other Settings

Configuring and Personalizing Chrome OS

Chrome OS works just fine in its default configuration. But there are a lot of things about Chrome you can configure to create a more uniquely personal user experience.

Personalizing the Desktop

You can customize the new Chrome OS desktop in terms of colors and background images. It's a quick and easy way to personalize your Chrome experience.

Change the Desktop Background

Most users like to select their own pictures for their computer desktops. It's no different with Chromebooks, which is why Chrome OS offers the option of personalized background images. You can select from images provided by Google, images uploaded from your computer, or plain colored backgrounds.

1. Click anywhere in the status area to display the Settings pane.

2. Click Settings.

3. Go to the Appearance section of the Settings page and click the Set Wallpaper button to open the Wallpaper window.

From the Desktop
You can also display the Wallpaper window by right-clicking (two-finger tap) anywhere on the open desktop and selecting Set Wallpaper.

4. Select a tab to display wallpapers of a given type—Nature, Urban, Colors, Landscape, or custom.

5. Click the wallpaper you want to use. This image is downloaded to your computer and set as your desktop background.

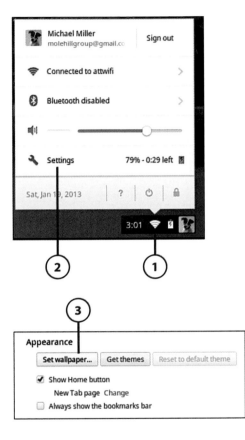

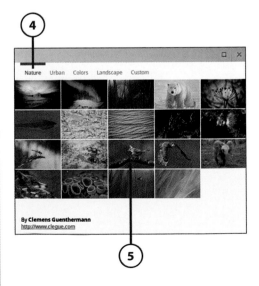

6. To select a solid color background, select the Colors tab and then click the desired color.

7. To upload your own personal image, select the Custom tab and then click the Choose File button. When the Select a File to Open window appears, navigate to and double-click the desired image file.

Fitting Custom Images

If you select a custom image that doesn't precisely fit the screen, use the Position menu to determine how that image is displayed—Center, Center Cropped, or Stretch.

Nature   Urban   **Colors**   Landscape   Custom

By **Google**
https://www.google.com/intl/en/chrome/device/

⑦   ⑥

Nature   Urban   Colors   Landscape   **Custom**

Custom Image:
[Choose File] Trains.jpg

Your wallpaper will be shown on the login screens and your background.

Position:
[Center Cropped ▼]

Preview:

Configuring the Chrome Browser

Because the Chrome browser is where you do most of your work, you probably want to take a few minutes to configure the browser to your personal preferences. You can change the home page displayed when the browser first launches; determine whether the Bookmarks bar is displayed; and change the entire look and feel of the browser by selecting a different theme.

Configure Startup Behavior

When you turn on your Chromebook and launch Chrome OS, one of three things can happen: Chrome can open the home page you set, reopen those pages that were open last, or open any pages you've preselected.

1. Click anywhere in the status area to display the Settings pane.

2. Click Settings.

Customize and Control

You can also open the Settings page by clicking the Customize and Control button at the top-right corner of the browser window.

3. Scroll to the bottom of the Settings page and click Show Advanced Settings.

4. To have Chrome open the default New Tab page on startup, go to the On Startup section and select the Open the New Tab Page option.

5. To have Chrome open the pages that were last open on startup, go to the On Startup section and select the Continue Where I Left Off option.

6. To have Chrome open pages you specify on startup, go to the On Startup section and select the Open a Specific Page or Set Pages option. Click Set Pages to display the Startup Pages pane and then enter the URL for the first page in the Add a New Page box. Press Enter to display an additional box, into which you can enter a second URL. Continue adding URLs as desired and then click OK.

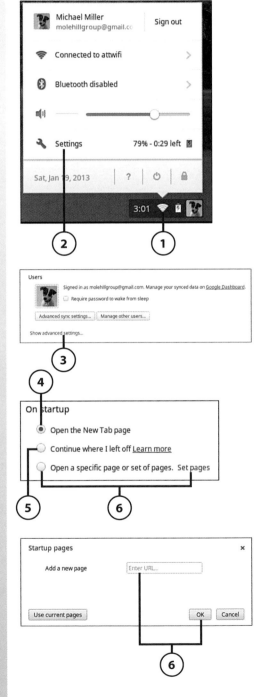

Use Current Pages

Another approach to specifying pages to open is to open the pages you want in separate browser tabs and then click the Use Current Pages button in the Startup Pages pane.

Display the Home Button

As described in the preceding section, you can configure Chrome to open a specific home page on startup. You can also display a Home button in the toolbar, next to the Omnibox; clicking this Home button displays the page you've set as your home page.

1. Click anywhere in the status area to display the Settings pane.

2. Click Settings.

3. Go to the Appearance section of the Settings page and check the Show Home Button option.

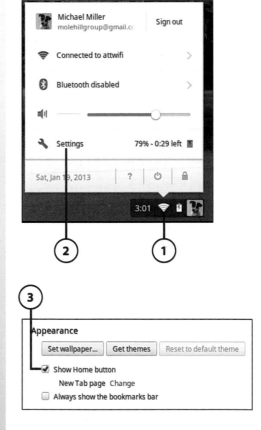

Display the Bookmarks Bar

Chrome enables you to store bookmarks to your favorite pages on the Bookmarks bar. This is a toolbar that displays beneath the normal Chrome toolbar. You can click a button on the Bookmarks bar to go directly to a bookmarked web page.

The Bookmarks bar displays automatically on the New Tab page. You can also opt to display the Bookmarks bar all the time in the Chrome browser.

1. Click anywhere in the status area to display the Settings pane.

2. Click Settings.

3. Go to the Appearance section of the Settings page and check the Always Show the Bookmarks Bar option.

Alternative Method

Alternatively, you can click the Customize and Control button in the top-right corner of the Chrome browser and then click Bookmarks, Show Bookmarks Bar.

Change Search Providers

Chrome's Omnibox functions both as an address box and a search box. That is, you can enter a search query into the Omnibox and your query is sent to your web search engine of choice.

Not surprisingly, Google is set as Chrome's default search engine provider. You can, however, opt to send your queries to any other search engine.

1. Click anywhere in the status area to display the Settings pane.

2. Click Settings.

3. Go to the Search section of the Settings page, click the first button (it should say "Google") and select a provider—Google, Yahoo!, or Bing.

4. Click the Manage Search Engines button to send your queries to a search engine that's not in the list of choices. When the Search Engines panel appears, make a selection from the Other Search Engines section, or enter the name and URL of a different search engine. After you've added the search engine, mouse over the search engine name and click the Make Default button.

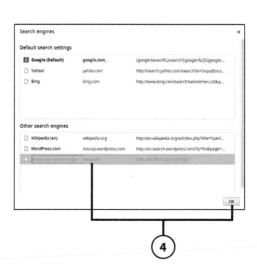

Enable Google Instant

When you're using Google's search engine, you can enable a new feature called Google Instant. This feature, not enabled by default, displays predicted search results as you type your query.

1. Click anywhere in the status area to display the Settings pane.

2. Click Settings.

3. Go to the Search section and check the Enable Instant for Faster Searching option in the Settings page.

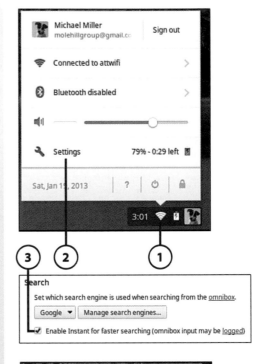

Select a New Theme

You can also change the look and feel of the Chrome browser window by selecting a new *theme*. A theme is a combination of colors, fonts, and background images; you can choose from any number of predesigned themes to personalize your browsing experience.

1. Click anywhere in the status area to display the Settings pane.

2. Click Settings.

3. Go to the Appearance section and click the Get Themes button on the Settings page. You connect to the Internet and go to the Themes section of the Chrome Web Store.

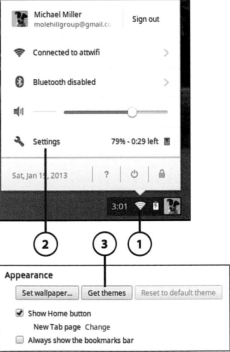

4. Search for themes (using the Search Themes box in the left sidebar) or browse through all available themes.

5. Click a theme thumbnail to view information about that theme.

6. Click the Choose Theme button to set the theme for your browser window.

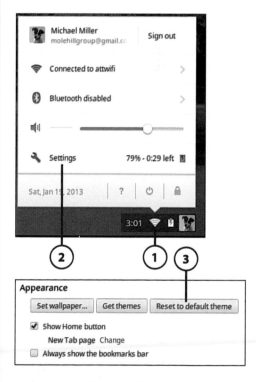

Reset to the Default Theme

You can return to Chrome's default theme at any time.

1. Click anywhere in the status area to display the Settings pane.

2. Click Settings.

3. Go to the Appearance section and click the Reset to Default Theme button on the Settings page.

DIFFERENT THEMES

Some themes affect mainly the color of the Chrome browser window. For example, the Glow theme turns the tabs and frame black and puts a nice glow behind the tabs. The Gradient theme, on the other hand, paints the entire browser window in a cool blue gradient.

Other themes have more of a graphical element. For example, the Space Planet theme puts a ringed alien planet background in the browser window, and the Dale Chihuly theme turns the entire browser into a dazzling display of colorful blown glass, just like a display by the famous artist.

Configuring Other Settings

There's more you can customize about Google Chrome, all accessible from the Settings page—which you get to by clicking anywhere in the status area and then clicking Settings. (Some settings might be visible only when you click Show Advanced Settings at the bottom of the page.)

Configure the Touchpad

Don't like the way your Chromebook's touchpad works or feels? Then change it.

1. To change the sensitivity of the touchpad, go to the Device section of the Settings pane and adjust the Touchpad Speed slider.

2. Change other touchpad functionality by clicking the Touchpad Settings button in the Device section.

3. To disable tap-to-click functionality (which then requires you to tap only at the bottom area of the touchpad), uncheck the Enable Tap-to-Click option and then click OK.

4. To scroll down a page by swiping downward on the touchpad, check the Enable Simple Scrolling option and then click OK.

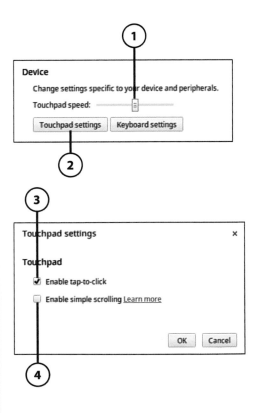

Change Search, Ctrl, and Alt Key Behavior

As previously noted, the Chromebook keyboard does not include some familiar keys, such as the Caps Lock key. You can, however, reconfigure how the Search, Ctrl, and Alt keys work in Chrome—and thus turn these keys into other keys that you might be missing.

Specifically, you can modify these keys as follows:

- **Search:** Change to Ctrl, Alt, Caps Lock, or disable.

- **Ctrl:** Change to Search, Alt, or disable.

- **Alt:** Change to Search, Ctrl, or disable.

1. Go to the Device section of the Settings pane and click the Keyboard Settings button.

2. Pull down the list for the key you want to modify and make a new selection.

3. Click the OK button.

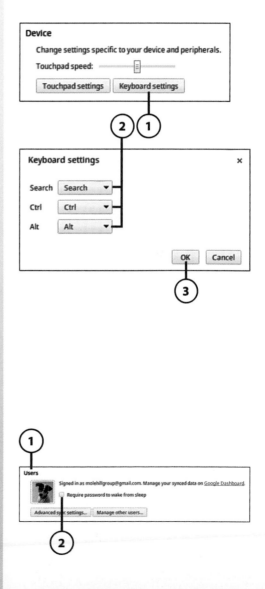

Wake from Sleep

If you want to keep strangers from accessing your Chromebook, you can require the entry of your user password whenever your device wakes from sleep mode. This is a nice bit of added security that ensures that nobody but you can access your running Chromebook and Google Account.

1. Scroll to the Users section of the Settings pane.

2. Check the Require Password to Wake from Sleep option.

Sync Your Account

Chrome OS and the Chrome browser are part of Google's web-based cloud computing architecture. As such, if you use the Chrome browser on multiple computers (even Windows or Mac machines), you can configure Chrome to use the same bookmarks and settings on those other PCs.

Synchronization

This synchronization between devices is possible because Google saves all your bookmarks and settings online in your Google Account. Whenever or wherever you launch Chrome and connect to your Google Account, the settings you see will be the same ones you saved previously. Any changes you make from any computer are also saved online, and those changes are visible from other computers you use to access the Internet. So after you get your Chromebook properly configured, the Chrome browser will look and feel the same on any other computer you use.

Synchronization is enabled by default on your Chromebook. You can, however, configure only certain settings to sync across all your computers.

1. Go to the Users section of the Settings pane and click the Advanced Sync Settings button.

2. Pull down the Sync Everything button and select either Sync Everything (default) or Choose What to Sync.

3. If you opted to choose what to sync, check any or all of the following items to synchronize: Apps, Autofill, Bookmarks, Extensions, Omnibox History, Passwords, Settings, Themes, or Open Tabs.

4. By default, Google automatically encrypts your account password for greater security. You can also opt to encrypt all the data synced in your Google Account by checking the Encrypt All Synced Data option.

5. Also by default, Google encrypts your passwords and data with your Google Account password. If you'd rather use a different password, select the Choose My Own Passphrase option and then enter and confirm the new password.

6. Click the OK button.

Advanced sync settings   ×

Sync everything ▼

☑ Apps   ☑ Extensions   ☑ Settings
☑ Autofill   ☑ Omnibox History ☑ Themes
☑ Bookmarks   ☑ Passwords   ☑ Open Tabs

Encrypted data types
For added security, Google Chrome will encrypt your data.
◉ Encrypt passwords
○ Encrypt all synced data

Encryption passphrase
◉ Use my Google Account password
○ Choose my own passphrase Learn more

Use default settings   OK   Cancel

Disable Guest Browsing

Guest browsing is enabled by default in Chrome. If you'd rather not have unregistered users using your Chromebook, you can disable the guest browsing feature.

1. Go to the Users section of the Settings pane and click the Manage Other Users button.

Users

Signed in as molehillgroup@gmail.com. Manage your synced data on Google Dashboard.
☐ Require password to wake from sleep

Advanced sync settings...   Manage other users...

2. Uncheck the Enable Guest
    Browsing box.

3. Click OK.

Owner-Only Settings

All settings that apply to other
users of your Chromebook
can only be configured by the
machine's owner.

Hide Usernames

By default, you see the usernames
and associated images for all users
added to your Chromebook. You
can, however, opt to hide these usernames and images.

1. Go to the Users section of the
    Settings pane and click the
    Manage Other Users button.

2. Uncheck the Show Usernames
    and Photos on the Sign-In Screen
    box.

3. Click OK.

Restrict Sign-In

Another option is to restrict sign-in to a list of preapproved users. This way only users you've okayed can sign into your Chromebook.

1. Go to the Users section of the Settings pane and click the Manage Other Users button.

2. Check the Restrict Sign-In to the Following Users option.

3. To add a user to the list, enter his or her username into the Add Users box and press Enter.

4. To delete a user from the approved list, click the X next to his or her name.

5. Click OK.

Change Your Time Zone

Chrome determines the current date and time over the Internet. However, it might not know your exact location—especially when you're traveling. Fortunately, it's easy to change the time zone displayed in Chrome.

1. Go to the Date and Time section of the Settings pane, pull down the Time Zone list, and select your current time zone.

2. By default, Chrome uses a standard AM/PM clock. If you'd rather use a 24-hour military clock, check the Use 24-Hour Clock box.

>>>Go Further

CONFIGURE PRIVACY OPTIONS

Privacy and security are important when you're browsing the web. To that end, Chrome includes a variety of privacy-related settings in the Privacy section of the Settings page. We discuss these settings in Chapter 14, "Using Google Chrome Safely and Securely." Turn there for more details.

Connect a Bluetooth Device

Many Chromebooks include built-in Bluetooth wireless, which is used to connect some wireless mice and keyboards. To connect an external Bluetooth device to your Chromebook, you first have to enable your device's Bluetooth functionality.

1. Go to the Bluetooth section of the Settings pane and check the Enable Bluetooth option to expand the section.

2. Click the Add a Device button to open the Add Bluetooth Device panel.

3. Your Chromebook searches for nearby Bluetooth devices. When the new device is found, highlight it in the list and click the Connect button.

4. Follow the onscreen instructions to connect your Bluetooth device. Enter a PIN for the connected device if you're prompted to do so.

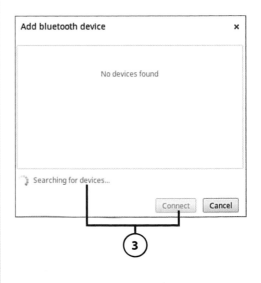

It's Not All Good

Bluetooth—or Not

If your Chromebook includes Bluetooth functionality, you'll see the Enable Bluetooth option on the Settings pane. If the Enable Bluetooth option isn't there, your Chromebook doesn't have built-in Bluetooth.

Enable Autofill

If you do a lot online shopping, you probably find yourself re-entering the same personal information on multiple shopping sites. You can simplify this data entry by enabling Chrome's Autofill feature, which stores your basic information and enters it automatically whenever you encounter a similar form on a web page.

1. Go to the Passwords and Forms section of the Settings pane and check the Enable Autofill option.

2. To view and manage your AutoFill settings, click Manage Autofill Settings. The Autofill Settings panel displays with your saved addresses and credit cards.

3. To delete an item, mouse over it and click the X button.

4. Click either the Add New Street Address or Add New Credit Card button to add a new item.

5. Click OK.

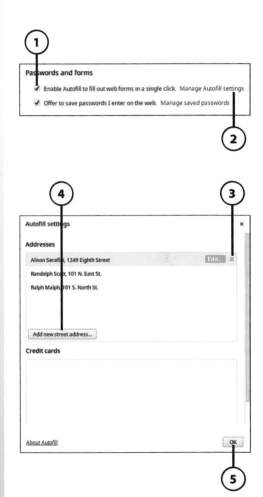

Passwords and forms

☑ Enable Autofill to fill out web forms in a single click. Manage Autofill settings

☑ Offer to save passwords I enter on the web. Manage saved passwords

Autofill settings   ✕

Addresses

Alison Serafin, 1249 Eighth Street   Edit... ✕

Randolph Scott, 101 N. East St.

Ralph Malph, 101 S. North St.

Add new street address...

Credit cards

About Autofill   OK

Save Passwords

By default, Chrome offers to save any passwords you enter when visiting web pages. This makes revisiting these pages that much faster and easier; Google enters the passwords for you, rather than you having to manually enter them yourself.

You can opt, however, for Google not to offer to save these passwords. This means you'll always have to enter required passwords manually—which makes for better security.

1. Go to the Passwords and Forms section of the Settings pane and uncheck the Offer to Save Passwords option.

2. To delete any saved passwords, click Manage Saved Passwords.

3. Sites where you've saved passwords are displayed at the top of the Passwords panel; sites where you've opted not to save passwords are listed at the bottom. Mouse over a site in the Saved Passwords section and click the X to delete that password from the list.

4. To change a password for a given site, mouse over the site and enter a new password into the box.

5. Click OK.

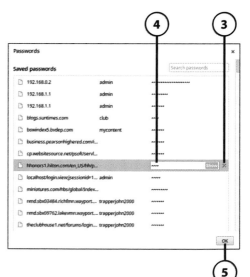

Display Web Content

Chrome offers several options that determine how web pages are displayed in the browser. In particular, you can change the size and type of fonts used, as well as change the zoom level when viewing pages.

1. To change the size of the fonts used to display web pages, go to the Web Content section of the Settings pane, pull down the Font Size list, and make a new selection from Very Small to Very Large. (Medium is the default size.)

2. To change the zoom level of the pages displayed, go to the Web Content section, pull down the Page Zoom list, and make a new selection.

3. To change the fonts used to display web pages, go to the Web Content section and click the Customize Fonts button.

4. To change the basic font, pull down the Standard Font list, make a new selection, and then adjust the slider to select the font size (from Tiny to Huge). To change the serif font used, pull down the Serif Font list and make a new selection. To change the sans serif font used, pull down the Sans-Serif Font list and make a new selection. To change the fixed-width font used, pull down the Fixed-Width Font list and make a new selection. To change the smallest size font displayed, adjust the Minimum Font Size slider.

5. Click OK.

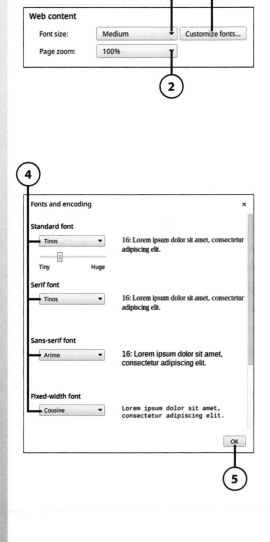

Customize Languages and Input Methods

By default, Chromebooks shipped in the U.S. display all menus and dialog boxes in English. If you speak another language, however, you can change this, and have Chrome display in a more familiar language.

You can also change the input method used for your Chromebook's keyboard. By default, Chrome uses a standard U.S. keyboard. You can opt instead to have your Chromebook mimic an international keyboard, extended keyboard, Dvoark keyboard, or Colemak keyboard.

1. Go to the Languages section of the Settings pane and click the Customize Languages and Input button.

2. Click the Add button in the Languages section to add another display language. When the next dialog box appears, click the language you want to use.

3. To change the keyboard input method, select another option from the Input Method section.

4. Click OK.

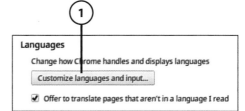

Languages

Change how Chrome handles and displays languages

Customize languages and input...

☑ Offer to translate pages that aren't in a language I read

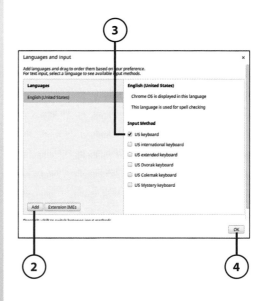

Languages and input

Add languages and drag to order them based on your preference.
For text input, select a language to see available input methods.

Languages

English (United States)

English (United States)

Chrome OS is displayed in this language

This language is used for spell checking

Input Method

☑ US keyboard

☐ US international keyboard

☐ US extended keyboard

☐ US Dvorak keyboard

☐ US Colemak keyboard

☐ US Mystery keyboard

Add   Extension IMEs

OK

Translate Pages

If you often run across web pages from other countries, and you don't know the language, you can configure Chrome to automatically translate foreign pages.

1. Go to the Languages section.

2. Check the Offer to Translate Pages option.

Languages

Change how Chrome handles and displays languages

Customize languages and input...

☑ Offer to translate pages that aren't in a language I read

Manage Downloads

When you download files from the Web, those files have to be stored somewhere. By default, that location is the Downloads folder—although that's something you can customize.

1. Go to the Downloads section of the Settings pane and click the Change button, and select a new folder.

2. If you want to be prompted for a new download location for each file, check the Ask Where to Save Each File option.

Downloads

Download location: Downloads   Change...

☑ Ask where to save each file before downloading

☐ Disable Google Drive on this device.

Disable Google Drive

Google Drive, Google's online storage service, shows up as a storage option when you're managing files on your Chromebook. You can, however, reconfigure Chrome so that you don't see Google Drive as an option.

1. Go to the Downloads section of the Settings pane.

2. Check the Disable Google Drive on This Device option.

Downloads

Download location: Downloads   [Change...]

☑ Ask where to save each file before downloading

☐ Disable Google Drive on this device.

>>>Go Further

MANAGE CLOUD PRINT

The Google Chrome OS does not enable printing directly from your Chromebook. Instead, you use Google's Cloud Print service to print to a printer connected to another computer. To learn more about configuring and using Cloud Print, turn to Chapter 13, "Printing with Google Cloud Print."

Enable Accessibility Features

If you have vision problems, using any operating system or web browser is difficult. Fortunately, Chrome includes several accessibility features that help you to find your way around the Chrome interface.

One of the most important accessibility features, especially for those with eyesight problems, is the ability to make the operating system speak to you. That is, Google's ChromeVox screenreader provides spoken feedback for all user actions. When ChromeVox is activated, all of Chrome's menus talk, and opening a web page produces a combination of spoken feedback and auditory cues. ChromeVox also includes a set of keyboard commands you can use to navigate Chrome menus and web pages.

ChromeVox

To learn more about the ChromeVox screenreader, go to www.chromevox.com.

1. To enable spoken feedback for user actions, go to the Accessibility section of the Settings pane and check the Enable Spoken Feedback option.

2. To display web pages with white type on a black background, go to the Accessibility section and check the Enable High Contrast Mode option.

3. To enlarge the screen so that smaller elements are easier to see, go to the Accessibility section and check the Enable Screen Magnifier option.

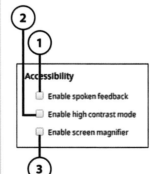

Online files via Google Drive

Local files

File Manager

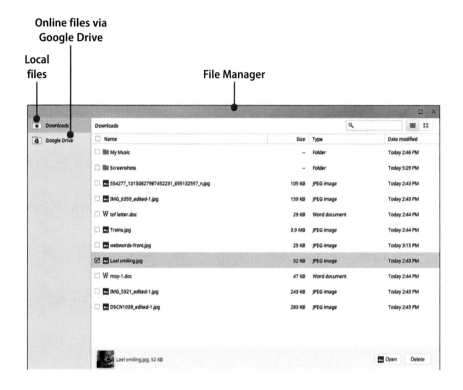

In this chapter, you find out how to manage stored and downloaded files on your Chromebook and on external devices connected to your Chromebook.

→ Using Chrome's File Manager
→ Using External Storage Devices

7

Managing Files and Using External Storage

Your Chromebook is designed to be a cloud-based computing device. That is, it's designed to work with web-based applications and files stored on the web. As such, most Chromebooks don't have much in the way of internal storage—a relatively meager 16MB of flash memory and no hard drive. (The big exception is the Acer C7 with its 320GB hard drive, which is big enough to store lots of big picture files.)

In addition to your Chromebook's internal storage, you can connect memory cards and USB memory devices to your Chromebook and use those devices for external storage. You manage these local files using Chrome's built-in File Manager. (And, of course, you can store anything you want online at Google Drive—which is covered in the next chapter.)

Using Chrome's File Manager

Chrome's File Manager is similar in concept to the file management utilities in the Windows and Mac operating systems. You can use the File Manager to view, open, copy, cut, paste, and delete files stored in your Chromebook's memory and on external devices connected to your Chromebook. It's relatively easy to access and, because of its limited functionality, quite easy to use.

To open the File Manager, press Ctrl+M on your Chromebook keyboard. You can also open the File Manager by clicking the Apps icon in the Launcher and selecting Files.

The File Manager itself consists of two sections. The sidebar, on the left, displays the three main types of storage on your Chromebook: Downloads (storage on the Chromebook itself), Google Drive (online storage with Google), and any external devices you have connected. The main part of the File Manager window displays the contents of the selected storage or folder.

The main window can display contents either as a list or as large thumbnails. You select the file view by clicking either the List View or Thumbnail View buttons at the top right of the File Manager window.

In List View, the contents of the selected folder are displayed by default in reverse chronological order—that is, the most recent files first. For each file, you see the filename, size, type, and date modified. You can sort by any of these attributes by clicking the top of the selected column.

In Thumbnail view, you see only the name of the file—along with a thumbnail image of the file's contents. For a picture file, the thumbnail is the picture itself. For other types of files, the thumbnail image is more generic, and sometimes reflective of the file type.

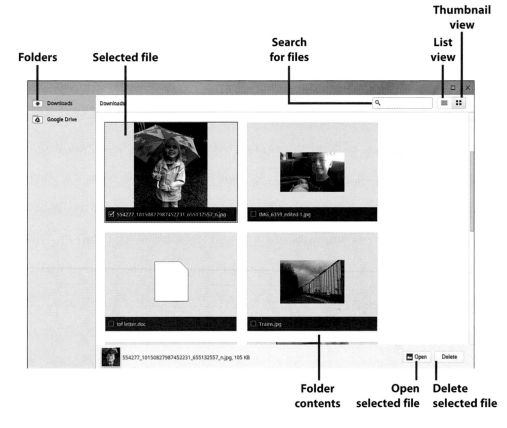

Thumbnail view

List view

Search for files

Folders **Selected file**

Folder contents **Open selected file** **Delete selected file**

At the top of the File Manager is a nested list of all the folders and subfolders in the path above the current folder. Click any folder or subfolder in this list to return directly to that folder.

Folders and subfolders (path)

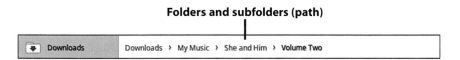

SUPPORTED FILE TYPES

>>>Go Further

Chrome can recognize many types of files, but not all. The following file types are officially recognized and supported by the Chrome OS:

- .bmp image files

- .doc and .docx Microsoft Word files (read-only)

- .gif image files

- .htm and .html web page files

- .jpg and .jpeg image files

- .mov video files

- .mp3 and .m4a audio files

- .mp4 and .m4v video files

- .ogv, .ogm, .ogg, and .oga Ogg Vorbis audio and video files

- .pdf Adobe Acrobat files

- .png image files

- .ppt and .pptx Microsoft PowerPoint files (read-only)

- .txt text files

- .wav audio files

- .webm video files

- .webp image files

- .xls and .xlsx Microsoft Excel files (read-only)

- .zip, .rar, .tar, .tar.gz, and tar.bz2 compressed files

You can store other file types on your Chromebook, or on external devices connected to your Chromebook, but you cannot open, view, or play other file types within Chrome.

Opening Files and Folders

There are several ways to open files and folders from within the File Manager.

1. Click the file or folder and then click the Open button at the bottom of the window.

2. Double-click the file or folder.

3. Right-click the file or folder and then select Open.

Office Files

If you try to open a Word, Excel, or PowerPoint file, File Manager displays a Chrome Office Viewer button instead of the normal Open button. Click this button to open the file in the Chrome Office View app.

Renaming Files and Folders

You can, if you wish, change the names of files from within the File Manager.

1. From within the File Manager, navigate to and right-click the file or folder you want to rename.

2. Select Rename from the pop-up menu.

Right-Clicking

To right-click using your Chromebook's touchpad, press the touchpad with two fingers.

3. The file or folder name is now highlighted. Type the new name into the highlighted area and press Enter.

Copying a File

It's relatively easy to copy a file from its current location to another folder on your Chromebook, to an external storage device, or to your Google Drive.

1. From within the File Manager, click to select the file you want to copy.
2. Right-click this file to display the pop-up menu.
3. Select Copy from the pop-up menu.
4. Navigate to and open the location where you want to copy the file.
5. Right-click an open area of the File Manager window to display the pop-up menu.
6. Click Paste.

Moving a File

Moving a file is different from copying it. When you copy a file, you leave that file in its original location, and paste a copy of that file to a new location; two files remain. When you move a file, via the cut-and-paste operation, the file is removed from its original location and pasted into the new location; only one file remains.

1. From within the File Manager, click to select the file you want to move.
2. Right-click this file to display the pop-up menu.
3. Select Cut from the pop-up menu.
4. Navigate to and open the location where you want to move the file.
5. Right-click an open area of the File Manager window to display the pop-up menu.
6. Click Paste.

Deleting Files

Naturally, you can use File Manager to delete files and folders. This is often necessary to free up the limited storage space on your Chromebook.

1. Navigate to and click the file(s) or folder(s) you want to delete.

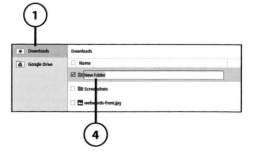

Selecting Multiple Files

You can select multiple files from within the File Manager. Just check the checkbox for each file you want to select, or hold down the Ctrl key while selecting multiple files.

2. Click the Delete button. Alternatively, you can right-click and select Delete from the pop-up menu.

Creating a New Folder

To better organize your stored files, you can use the File Manager to create multiple folders and subfolders.

1. Navigate to the folder where you want to add the new subfolder.

2. Right-click anywhere in an open area of the File Manager window to display the pop-up menu.

3. Click New Folder.

4. File Manager creates the new folder with the name area open for editing. Enter a name for the new folder and press Enter.

Saving Files from the Web

Often you'll find images and other files on websites that you'd like to save copies of. You can save these files directly to your Chromebook, or to a memory card or external USB memory device connected to your Chromebook.

Limited Storage

Because your Chromebook has limited storage on board, you should probably save most downloaded files to an external storage device or to your Google Drive.

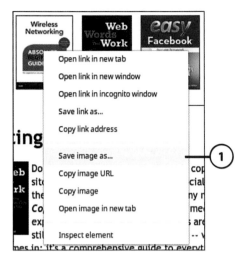

1. From within the Chrome browser, right-click the file or image you want to save and then select Save Image As or Save File As from the pop-up menu.

2. When the Save File As window appears, select a folder in which to save the file.

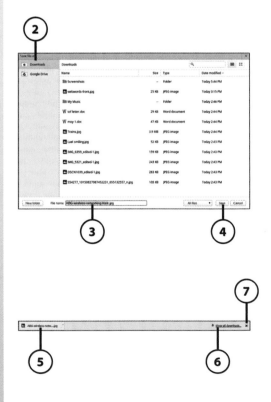

3. Confirm or change the name of the file in the File Name field.

4. Click the Save button.

5. Chrome displays the Downloads pane at the bottom of the browser window, with a button for the selected file on the far left. To view the downloaded file, click the file button.

6. Click the Show All Downloads link to view all recently downloaded files.

7. Click the X at the far right to close the downloads pane.

Using External Storage Devices

You can connect various types of external file storage to your Chromebook. In particular, you can connect USB memory devices, memory cards (such as those used in digital cameras), and any external hard drive that connects via USB.

Connecting a USB Memory Device

You can connect any USB memory device (sometimes called a flash drive or thumb drive) to your Chromebook's USB ports and then access data stored on the drive using Chrome's File Manager.

1. Insert the USB memory device into an open USB port on your Chromebook.

2. Chrome recognizes the USB device, opens the File Manager, and displays the contents of the device.

Inserting a Memory Card

Your Chromebook's Multi-Card slot can read and write data to and from popular types of memory cards. The Samsung Chromebook reads/writes SD (Secure Digital), SDHC (Secure Digital High Capacity), SDXC (Secure Digital Extended Capacity), and MMC (MultiMediaCard) cards. The Acer C7 Chromebook reads/writes SD and MMC cards.

These memory cards are typically used to store images taken from digital cameras. When you insert a memory card into your Chromebook, you can view the images stored on the card. You can also use memory cards to store files downloaded from the Internet.

1. Insert the memory card into the memory card slot on your Chromebook.

2. Chrome recognizes the memory card, opens the File Manager, and displays the contents of the card.

Screen Captures

If you need to capture a picture of the current screen on your Chromebook, press the Ctrl+Next Window button. Screen captures are stored in the File Shelf, Screenshots folder.

Connecting an External Hard Drive

Current-generation Chromebooks also let you use external USB hard drives for additional storage. This way, you can store more and larger files than you can with the Chromebook's internal storage; you can also use the external hard drive to store backup copies of your most important files.

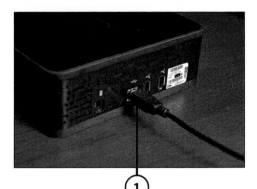

1. Connect one end of a USB cable to the USB connector on the external hard drive.

2. Connect the other end of the USB cable to an open USB port on your Chromebook.

3. Chrome recognizes the external drive, opens the File Manager, and displays the contents of the drive.

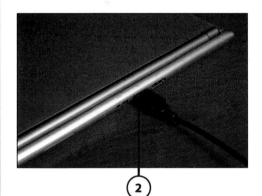

Google Drive
online storage

In this chapter, you find out how to store your important files on the Web using Google Drive.

→ Getting Started with Google Drive
→ Storing Files on Google Drive
→ Sharing Google Drive Files

Using Google Drive to Store and Share Files

Most Chromebooks have minimal onboard storage space for files, and Chrome OS itself was built on the concept of cloud-based file storage. When it comes to storing your files online, Google recommends its Google Drive cloud storage service. Google Drive makes it easy to access your important files from any computer, in any location. Google Drive is also great for sharing files with friends, family, and co-workers.

Getting Started with Google Drive

Google Drive appears as a storage device in your Chromebook's File Manager. You can copy files to and from Google Drive as you would to and from any storage device or location.

File Manager

Learn more about using Chrome's File Manager in Chapter 7, "Managing Files and Using External Storage."

Configure Google Drive

Several Chromebook manufacturers offer their users 100GB of free Google Drive storage for two years. Even if you aren't offered or don't take advantage of the 100GB promotion, you still get 5GB of free storage; additional space is available, for a fee. You set up your Google Drive account the first time you select Google Drive in the File Manager.

1. Press Ctrl+M to open the File Manager.

2. Click Google Drive in the sidebar to connect to your Google Drive account.

3. Click the Get Started button. Your Chrome browser opens and displays a Google Drive welcome page.

4. If your Chromebook comes with a 100GB free storage offer, click the Redeem Offer button.

Free Gogo Passes

For a limited time, you also get 12 free Gogo in-air Internet passes that you can use for the next two years on domestic U.S. flights. You redeem these passes from the same page where you redeem your 100GB Google Drive offer.

5. Click the Allow button to verify that you're using an eligible Chrome OS device.

6. Click Start Using Google Drive.

    Google displays the main Google Drive page (drive.google.com).

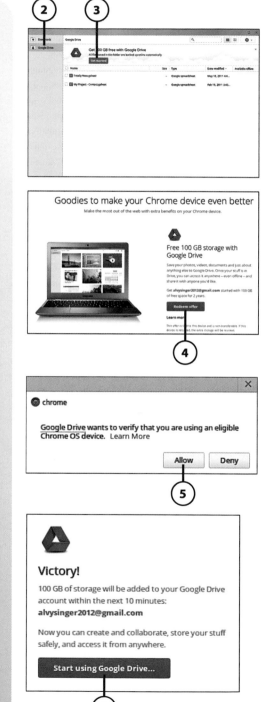

Storing Files on Google Drive

Although you can manage your Google Drive files from the Google Drive web page (drive.google.com), it's easier to do it from within Chrome's File Manager.

View Your Google Drive Files

When you first sign up for Google Drive, you see a few "test" files in your main folder. You can delete these if you want and then begin using Google Drive to store additional files.

1. Click Google Drive in the sidebar of File Manager. The contents of your main folder display; different types of files have their own distinctive icons.

2. Click any subfolder to view its contents.

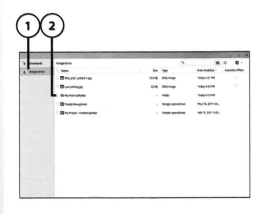

Copy a File to Google Drive

Copying a file from your Chromebook or external storage device is as easy as clicking and dragging.

1. From within File Manager, select the file you want to copy to Google Drive.

2. Click and drag the file to the Google Drive icon in the sidebar.

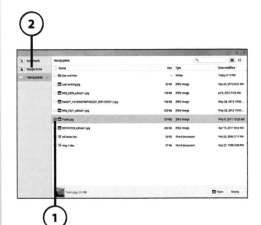

Copy and Paste
You can also copy a file to your Google Drive by right-clicking the file and selecting Copy; you then open your Google Drive folder, right-click, and select Paste.

Open a File from Google Drive

Opening a file stored on Google Drive is just like opening a file stored directly on your Chromebook.

1. Click Google Drive in the sidebar of File Manager and then navigate to the file you want to open.

2. Click to select the file you want to open.

3. Click the Open button at the bottom of the File Manager window.

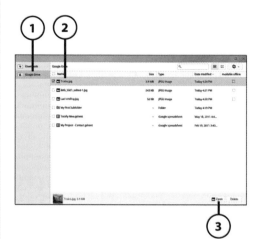

Delete Files from Google Drive

From time to time, it's good to free up space in your Google Drive folder by deleting old or unused files.

1. Click Google Drive in the sidebar of File Manager and then navigate to the file(s) you want to delete.

2. Click to select the file(s) you want to delete.

3. Click the Delete button at the bottom of the File Manager window.

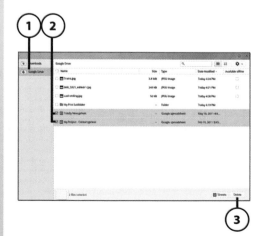

Create a New Google Drive Folder

To better organize large numbers of files, you can create additional subfolders within your main Google Drive folder. You can then use these subfolders to store specific types of files. For example, you might create a subfolder just for work files, or for holiday pictures.

1. Click Google Drive in the sidebar of File Manager and then navigate to where you want to create the new subfolder.

2. Right-click anywhere in an open area of the File Manager window to display the pop-up menu and then click New Folder.

3. Google Drive creates the new folder with the name area open for editing. Enter a name for the new folder and press Enter.

Sharing Google Drive Files

Google Drive cloud storage is ideal for when you want to share a file with someone. Perhaps you want to share pictures with friends or family, or even collaborate on a group project for work. All you have to do is tell Google Drive to share that file with selected people and then they can view it from their own computers or smartphone. (Or, if you enable the proper access, edit the file, too.)

Share a File with Selected Users

Unfortunately, you can't configure files for sharing from within File Manager. To share files, you have to go to the Google Drive website.

1. From within File Manager, select Google Drive, click the Gear button, and then click Go to drive. Alternatively, go to drive.google.com to open Google Drive in a Chrome browser window.

2. Navigate to and select the file you want to share.

3. Click the Share button to display the Sharing Settings pane.

4. By default, all your files are private, except for the people you specify. To share the file with a person, enter his or her Google Account username or standard email address into the Add People box.

5. Pull down the list to the right of the Add People box and select Can Edit to make the file editable by the people you are sharing with.

6. Pull down the list to the right of the Add People box and select Can Connect to let collaborators view and comment on the file (but not edit it).

7. Pull down the list to the right of the Add People box and select Can View to make the file read only (that is, no one but you can edit it).

8. Click the Share & Save button.

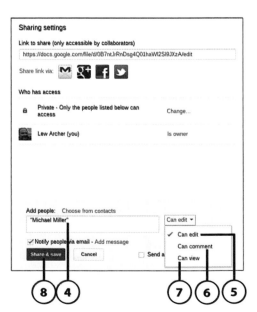

Share a File via Social Media or Gmail

Google Drive also enables you to share selected files with your Facebook, Twitter, and Google+ followers and friends. This is a great way to share your favorite pictures with large groups of people.

1. From the Google Drive web page, navigate to and select the file you want to share.

2. Click the Share button to display the Sharing Settings pane.

3. Click the icon for Gmail or the social network on which you want to share this file.

4. Complete the onscreen instructions to share this file on the selected social network and then click the Share To button.

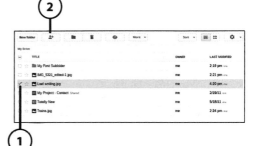

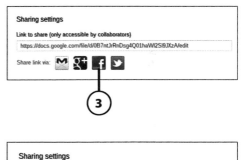

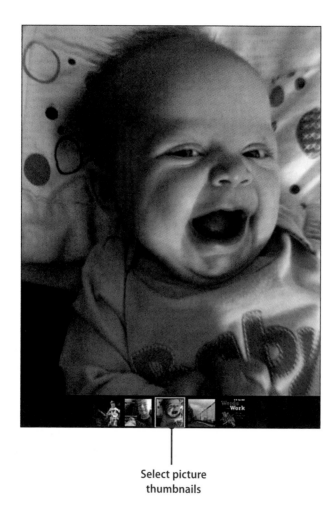

Select picture
thumbnails

In this chapter, you find out how to view and listen to various types of media files on your Chromebook.

→ Viewing Digital Photos on Your Chromebook
→ Listening to Music on Your Chromebook
→ Watching Videos on Your Chromebook

Viewing and Listening to Photos, Videos, and Music

Many people use their computers and tablets to view and listen to a variety of media files—photos, music, and videos. Not surprisingly, you can use your Chromebook as a photo viewer and media player, as long as you work within Chrome's storage and file format limitations.

That is, you have to figure out some way to store large media files *not* on the Chromebook itself—or stream your audio and video over the Internet, in real time. And you have to make sure that all your media files are in a format that is supported by Google Chrome.

Viewing Digital Photos on Your Chromebook

Your Chromebook is the perfect device for viewing your digital photos. Fortunately, Google Chrome is compatible with most major image formats, including the .jpg, .gif, .png, and .bmp file formats.

View Photos from an External Storage Device

Because your Chromebook's internal storage is limited, the best way to view digital photos is to first store them on an external storage device, such as a memory card or USB memory device. You can then insert the external storage device into your Chromebook to view the photos.

1. Insert the external storage device into your Chromebook.

2. When File Manager opens, open the folder for the external storage device and navigate to the folder where the photos are stored.

3. Click the image file you want to view, or select the item and click the Open button. The selected image opens in Chrome's photo viewer.

4. Mouse over the viewer to see the navigation controls. Click the right arrow to advance to the next photo, or the left arrow to display the previous photo.

5. Click the Slideshow button to display all the photos in the folder in a full-screen slideshow.

6. Click the Delete button to delete the current picture.

7. Click the X at the top-right corner of the window to close the photo viewer.

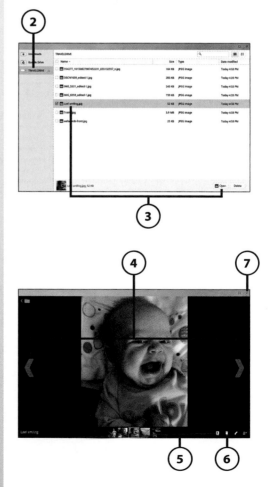

Edit a Photo

Chrome's photo viewer also includes basic photo editing functionality. You can use the photo viewer to crop a picture, adjust brightness, rotate the picture 90° right or left, or apply a general "auto-fix" option that attempts to correct contrast, brightness, and color issues.

1. Open the picture you want to edit in Chrome's photo viewer.

2. Mouse over the picture and then click the Edit button to display the editing controls.

3. Click Auto-fix to apply an automatic fix to the picture.

4. Click Left to rotate the picture 90° counterclockwise.

5. Click Right to rotate the picture 90° clockwise.

6. Click Crop and then drag the corners of the crop box as needed. Press Enter when you're done.

7. Click Brightness and then adjust the Brightness and Contrast sliders. Your changes are saved automatically.

8. Click the Edit button to exit photo editing mode.

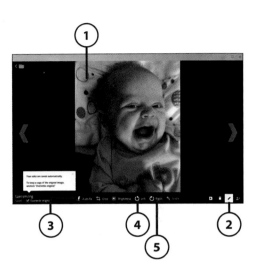

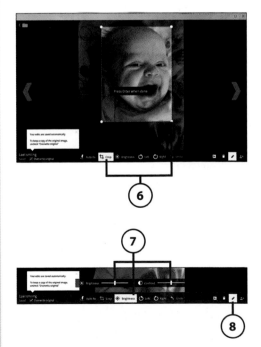

Store and Share Photos Online with Picasa Web Albums

If you want to store more photos than you have space for locally, consider using Google's Picasa Web Albums. This free service, tied into your Google Account, lets you store your photos online and then share them with friends and family.

1. Open the Chrome browser, go to picasaweb.google.com, and log in with your Google account.

2. Click the Upload button to upload new photos.

3. Your photos are organized into albums. Click an album's thumbnail to view the contents of that album.

4. Click a picture's thumbnail to view that picture.

5. To share the contents of the current album, click Actions, Album Properties to display the Edit Album Information pane. Click the Visibility button and select either Public on the Web or Limited, Anyone with the Link.

6. Click the Save Changes button.

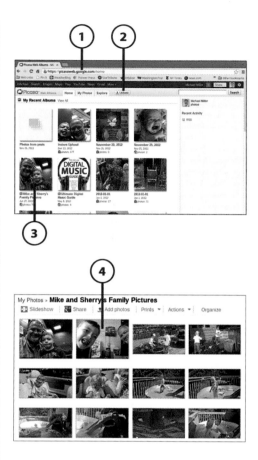

Listening to Music on Your Chromebook

If you want to listen to music on your Chromebook, you're in luck. Chrome includes its own Audio Player application, which you can use both to listen to tunes and watch videos.

As with viewing photos, your Chromebook's storage limitations makes it difficult to store large numbers of music files internally. Your better bet is to transfer the desired music files to a USB memory device and then insert that device into your Chromebook. You can then listen to the files stored on the USB device, using Chrome's Audio Player.

Note, however, that Chrome's Audio Player does not support all types of music files. It's compatible with the popular MP3 audio format, but not with Apple's .aac or Microsoft's .wma formats. So if you have your files in an iTunes library, for example, you first need to convert them to MP3 format to listen to on your Chromebook.

Listen to a Single Track

We'll assume that you've already copied your favorite MP3 files to a USB memory device. You use that device to listen to your music on your Chromebook.

1. Insert the external storage device into your Chromebook.

2. When File Manager opens, open the folder for the external storage device and navigate to the folder where the MP3 files are stored.

3. Click the music file to which you want to listen. Alternatively, you can select the file and then click the Listen button. The Audio Player opens and starts playback.

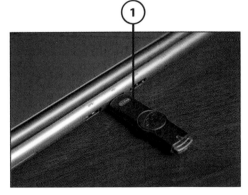

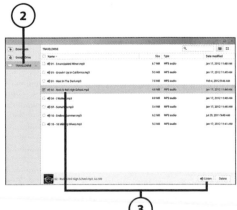

4. Click the Pause button to pause playback; to resume playback, click the Play button.

5. Click the X at the upper-right corner to close the Audio Player.

Listen to a Playlist

Chrome's Audio Player can also play back a playlist of multiple tracks. This lets you program music for an extended sitting.

1. Open File Manager and check those music files you want to include in the playlist.

2. Click the Listen button in the Preview pane to open the Audio Player and start playback of the first song in the playlist.

3. Click the Pause button to pause playback; to resume playback, click the Play button.

4. Click the Next Track button to advance to the next song in the playlist.

5. Click the Previous Track button to listen to the previous song.

6. Click the Playlist button to view the entire playlist. The Audio Player pane expands to display all tracks in the playlist.

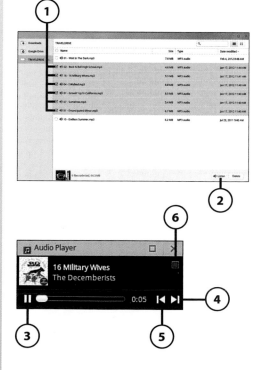

Uploading Your Music to Google Play

Listening to your own music via an external storage device might not be ideal for all users. Many music lovers prefer to listen to streaming music over the Internet; this provides for a larger selection of music with no local storage limitations.

To this end, Google offers the Google Play music service, which enables you to stream your own music back to you over the Internet. You can upload the favorite tracks from your personal music collection and then play them back from any web browser—including the Chrome browser on your Chromebook. You can upload and listen to up to 20,000 individual tracks, all for free.

Scan and Match
Google Play is actually a "scan and match" music service. That is, it scans the files you want to upload and then matches them against tracks in its own large music library. If the tracks are already there, it doesn't have to upload your tracks, thus saving you lots of time. If, on the other hand, your tracks are not in Google's library, it uploads them for your future listening pleasure.

Unfortunately, you can't upload music directly from your Chromebook to Google Play. Instead, you need to have your digital music stored on a Windows or Mac PC, and then use that machine for uploading. You'll first need to install Google's Music Manager application on your PC; go to play.google.com/music/listen and click the Upload Music button. You can then select which files to upload to your Google Play music library.

File Formats
Google's Music Manager lets you upload audio files in the following audio formats: .mp3, .m4a/AAC, .wma (Windows only), .flac, and .ogg.

1. Launch the Music Manager app from your Windows or Mac PC and select the Upload tab.

2. Click the Add Folder button and then browse to and select the folder where you store your digital music.

3. Click the Upload button to upload all the tracks in this folder.

4. Check the Automatically Upload Songs option if you want to automatically upload new tracks you add to this folder.

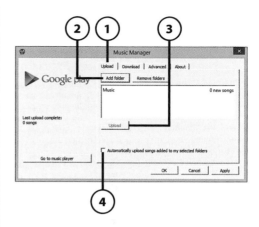

Uploading from Your Chromebook

Although music uploading is not possible by default in Chrome OS, the third-party MusicAlpha app adds uploading for MP3 files stored either on your Chromebook or an external storage device. Note, however, that the app is still in its testing phase, and does not appear to work for all users. If you're interested, go to the Chrome Web Store and search for MusicAlpha.

Playing Music with Google Play

After you've uploaded your music to Google Play , you can use your Chromebook's Chrome browser to play back your favorite tracks.

1. Click Apps in the Launcher and then click Google Play Music. Alternatively, open the Chrome browser and go to play.google.com/music/listen. Google Play opens in the Chrome browser.

2. Use the navigation sidebar to select what you want to listen to—Songs, Artists, Albums, Genres, or specific playlists.

3. Select the playlist, album, or songs you want to listen to. (Hold down the Ctrl button to select multiple tracks.)

4. Click the Play button to begin playback.

5. Click the Shuffle button to play your selections in a random order.

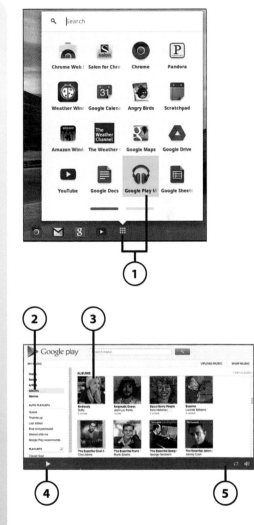

>>>Go Further

STREAMING MUSIC SERVICES

There are several web-based services that stream music to any connected device over the Internet. These streaming music services typically offer tens of millions of tracks for your listening pleasure, either for free or a low monthly subscription fee. Many offer Chrome apps for their services; those that don't have apps can be accessed from the Chrome web browser.

The most popular streaming music services among Chromebook users include the following:

- Earbits Radio (www.earbits.com)
- iHeartRadio (www.iheart.com)
- Listen Radio Online (online-radio.appspot.com)
- Mixcloud (www.mixcloud.com)
- MOG (www.mog.com)
- Pandora (www.pandora.com)
- Radio Paradise HD (www.radioparadise.com)
- Rdio (www.rdio.com)
- TuneYou Radio (www.tuneyou.com)

Also popular are Last.fm (www.last.fm) and Slacker Radio (www.slacker.com). Although these services don't have Chrome apps, you can still listen to them in your Chrome browser. (Spotify, another popular streaming music service, requires installation of its own music player program and is not compatible with Chromebooks.)

Watching Videos on Your Chromebook

You can use your Chromebook to watch movies, TV shows, and home movies, stored either internally or externally. You can also stream movies and TV shows over the Internet and view them in the Chrome browser.

View a Video

If you have home movies or other videos on some sort of external storage device, you can easily view them on your Chromebook—as long as the individual video is in an approved file format. At present, Chrome supports videos encoded in the .mp4, .mpv,.mov, and .webm file formats, as well as Ogg Vorbis video files.

WebM

WebM is a new video file format promoted by Google. It is likely that Google will adopt WebM as the video file format of choice for all of its video-related websites, including YouTube.

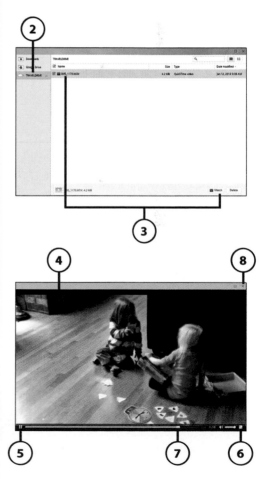

1. Insert the external storage device into your Chromebook.

2. When File Manager opens, open the folder for the external storage device and navigate to the subfolder where the video file is stored.

3. Click the video file you want to view. Alternatively, select the video file and click the Watch button. The video begins playback in the Media Player window.

4. Mouse over the video to display the transport controls.

5. Click the Pause button to pause playback; to resume playback, click the Play button.

6. Click the Fullscreen button to view the video full screen on your desktop.

7. Drag the slider to the right (forward) or the left (backward) to advance to another section of the video.

8. Click the X at the top-right corner to close the Media Player window.

Watch TV Shows on Hulu

The most popular site for watching TV shows online is Hulu (www.hulu.com). Hulu offers a good selection of TV shows for free, and an even better selection with its $7.99/month Hulu Plus service. You watch Hulu videos in the Chrome web browser.

It's Not All Good

No Netflix

Netflix (www.netflix.com) is perhaps the most popular online streaming movie service. Unfortunately, it does not currently work with Chromebooks and the Chrome OS. Check with the Netflix site for updates on this situation.

1. Open the Chrome browser, go to www.hulu.com, and sign into your account.

2. Search or browse for the program you want to watch. In many instances, you have the option of accessing complete seasons or individual episodes.

3. Click the thumbnail of the program you want to watch. Playback begins.

4. Mouse over the browser window to display the playback controls.

5. Click the Full Screen button to view the program full-screen on your desktop.

6. Click the Pause button to pause playback; click the Play button to resume playback.

7. Use the playback slider to advance through the program.

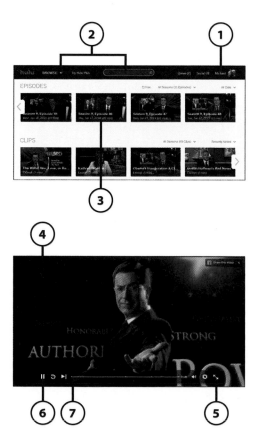

Watch YouTube Videos

Google also makes it easy to watch videos from its YouTube subsidiary. YouTube (www.youtube.com) contains millions of videos uploaded by both companies and individuals; it's a great place to find just about anything in video format, and it's totally free.

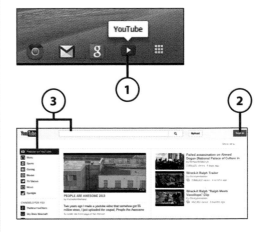

1. Click the YouTube button in the Chrome Launcher, or use the Chrome browser to go to www.youtube.com. The YouTube home page displays.

2. Click the Sign In button to sign into your account.

3. Browse or search for a video you want to watch.

4. Click the video's thumbnail to begin playback on a new page.

5. Click Pause to pause playback; click Play to resume playback.

6. Click anywhere on the red slider to move to a different place in the video.

7. Click the Full Screen button to view the video full screen.

Vimeo

Vimeo (www.vimeo.com) is another popular video-sharing website. There's a nice Vimeo app in the Chrome Web Store that many Chromebook users seem to like.

Web
page   Tab   Omnibox   Settings
                                                              menu

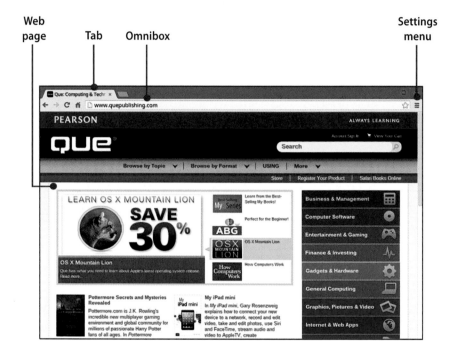

In this chapter, you find out how to use Google Chrome to browse and search the Web.

- → Browsing the Web
- → Viewing and Managing Browser History
- → Searching the Web
- → Managing Your Home Page
- → Bookmarking Favorite Pages
- → Browsing in Incognito Mode

Browsing and Searching the Web

The Google Chrome OS is built around Google's Chrome web browser. Chrome (the browser) is similar to other web browsers available today, but with a sleeker interface—there's no menu bar, search bar, or status bar, as older browsers tend to have. This difference makes the web page bigger in the browser window, and it simplifies the browsing experience. In essence, Chrome moves the business of the browser out of the way so that you can pay more attention to the web page itself.

Browsing the Web

Google's Chrome web browser is integrated into the Chrome OS interface. You use the Chrome browser to access all web-based apps, as well as most system settings.

The Chrome browser resembles Internet Explorer, Firefox, and other modern web browsers, complete with tabs for different web pages. To go to a web page, type the page's address (also called a URL) into the Omnibox at the top of the Chrome window; the web page displays in the current tab.

Tab   Omnibox

Go to a Web Page

One of the quickest ways to browse the Web is to go directly to a given web page. You do this by entering the page's address, or URL, into Chrome's Omnibox.

Omnibox

What others call an Address box, Chrome calls the Omnibox. That's because it's more than a simple address box; you can also use it to enter queries for web searches. When you start typing in the Omnibox, Google suggests both likely web pages and search queries. Just select what you want from the list or finish typing your URL or query, and then press Enter.

1. Type a web page's URL into the Omnibox at the top of the Chrome window.

2. Google suggests both likely queries and web pages you are likely to visit. Select the page you want from the drop-down list.

Or

3. Finish typing your URL and press Enter.

Chrome navigates to and displays the page you entered.

Click Links

Another way to navigate the Web is to click links to other pages you find on web pages. Clicking a link takes you directly to the linked-to page; you can open links in the current browser tab or, if you prefer to keep the current page visible, in a new tab or window.

1. To open the link in the current tab, click the link.

2. To open the link in a new tab, right-click the link and select Open Link in New Tab.

3. To open the link in a new window, right-click (tap with two fingers) the link and select Open Link in New Window.

Reload a Page

If you stay on a web page too long, you might miss updates to that page's content. In addition, if a page doesn't fully or properly load, you might need to "refresh" or reload that page.

1. Click the Reload This Page button to the left of the address bar.

Move Forward and Back Through Pages

You can easily revisit pages you've previously displayed and then move forward again through visited pages.

1. Click the Back button to move backward through previously visited pages.

2. Click the Forward button to move forward through pages.

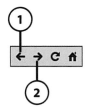

Zoom into a Page

If you're having trouble reading small text on a page, Chrome lets you increase the zoom level to make that text bigger. You can also decrease the zoom level to make the entire page smaller.

1. Click the Customize and Control button at the top right to display the drop-down menu.

2. To increase the zoom level, go to the Zoom section of the menu and click the + button.

3. To decrease the zoom level, go to the Zoom section of the menu and click the – button.

Viewing and Managing Browser History

Another way to revisit web pages you have viewed in the past is to use Google Chrome's history feature. Chrome keeps track of your history for up to ten weeks.

View Your Recent History

1. Click and hold the Back button to display a list of pages you've visited in your current browsing session.

2. To revisit a specific page, click it in the list.

① **②**

← → C ⌂ 🔒 https://www.google.com

🅑 Ultimate Digital Music Guide
🅑 Mike and Sherry's Family Pictures
🅟 Que: Computing & Technology Books, Video, Articles for Home & Business
🅖 Google
🗋 New Tab

🕓 Show Full History

View Your Full History

To revisit pages viewed on other days, you can access your full browsing history.

1. Click the Customize and Control button to display the drop-down menu.

2. Click History. The History page displays in a new tab.

3. To revisit any particular page, click that page's link.

More History
To view additional pages in your history, scroll to the bottom of the page and click the Older link.

4. To search for a particular page you've visited, enter that page's name or URL into the search box and click the Search History button.

☆ **☰** ①

New tab	Ctrl+T
New window	Ctrl+N
New incognito window	Ctrl+Shift+N
Bookmarks	▶

| Edit | | Cut | Copy | Paste |

Save page as...	Ctrl+S
Find...	Ctrl+F
Print...	Ctrl+P

| Zoom | – | 100% | + | ⌞ ⌝ |

| History | Ctrl+H | ② |
| Downloads | Ctrl+J |

④   **③**

History   Search history

Clear all browsing data...   Remove selected items

Today - Wednesday, January 23, 2013

5:52 PM 🅖 Google www.google.com
5:52 PM 🅑 Ultimate Digital Music Guide ultimatedigitalmusicguide.blogspot.com
5:52 PM 🅑 Mike and Sherry's Family Pictures ★ mikeandsherrypictures.blogspot.com
5:51 PM 🅟 Que: Computing & Technology Books, Video, Articles for Home & Business ★ www.quepublishing.com
5:51 PM 🗋 Michael Miller: The Molehill Group ★ www.molehillgroup.com
5:50 PM 📘 Easy Computer Basics, Windows 8 Edition: Michael Miller: 9780789750051: Amazon.co... www.amazon.com
5:37 PM ▶ High Definition Videos for YouTube - YouTube www.youtube.com
5:36 PM ▶ michael miller trapperjohn2000 - YouTube www.youtube.com
5:36 PM ▶ Que Publishing - YouTube www.youtube.com
5:36 PM ▶ Que Publishing - YouTube www.youtube.com
5:36 PM ▶ que publishing - YouTube www.youtube.com

Delete Browsing History

You might not want your entire browsing history visible to others using your Chromebook—or accessing your Chrome browser on another computer. To that end, you can delete your browsing history—as well as other "tracks" to your web browsing.

Chrome enables you to do any and all of the following:

- Delete browsing history (web pages you've visited)

- Delete download history (files you've downloaded)

- Empty the cache

- Delete cookies and other site data

- Clear saved passwords

- Clear saved Autofill form data

Cache

The *cache* is a local storehouse of recently visited pages. By accessing cached pages, Chrome can reload these pages faster.

Cookies

A cookie is a small text file, stored on your computer, that certain websites use to track your browsing behavior. Cookies are sometimes used to record personal data to facilitate future visits; they're also sometimes used to serve up relevant web ads.

You can clear any of these items stored in the past hour, the past day, the past week, the past four weeks, or from the beginning of time (or at least when you started using your Chromebook).

It's Not All Good

Why Not to Clear Browsing Data

You might not want to select all the options in the Clear Browsing Data dialog box. Clearing browsing and download data erases your browsing history, so those are probably good choices. Emptying the cache is sometimes necessary, in and of itself, to clear out old versions of pages and enable you to see the most recent versions of some web pages. Deleting cookies is generally not advised, however, as this will get rid of tracking data that make some sites easier to access. And clearing saved passwords and Autofill form data might also make it less convenient to revisit pages where you've previously entered information.

1. Click the Customize and Control button to display the drop-down menu.

2. Select More Tools, Clear Browsing Data to display the Clear Browsing Data dialog box.

3. Check those items you want to delete or clear.

4. Pull down the Obliterate the Following Items From list and select how much data to delete: past hour, past day, past week, last 4 weeks, or from the beginning of time.

5. Click the Clear Browsing Data button.

Searching the Web

As mentioned previously, Google Chrome's Omnibox functions not only as an address box but also as a search box for searching the Web. That is, you can also use the Address box to enter a search query and send your search to Google or another search engine.

Enter a Query

You use the Omnibox to enter search queries that are then sent to your favorite web search engine. By default, your queries are sent to Google, so it should be a familiar experience.

1. Enter your search query into the Omnibox at the top of the browser window.

2. Google suggests both likely queries and web pages you are likely to visit in a drop-down list. Select the query you want from the drop-down list.

   Or

3. Finish typing your query and then press Enter.

   Your search results are now displayed in the browser window.

Google Search Page

You can also, of course, do your searching from Google's main search page on the Web (www.google.com)—but you get the exact same results as you do when searching from Chrome's Omnibox.

Using Google Search

Learn more about searching with Google in my companion ebook, *Using Google Advanced Search* (Michael Miller, Que, 2011).

Use Google Instant

Google is always striving to simplify the search process and provide better results, faster. To this end, the company recently introduced a new featured dubbed Google Instant. When activated, Google Instant displays predicted search results on the search page as you type, instead of waiting for you to click the Google Search button. These instant search results can save time and help you fine-tune your query as you're typing it.

New tab			Ctrl+T
New window			Ctrl+N
New incognito window		Ctrl+Shift+N	
Bookmarks			▶
Edit	Cut	Copy	Paste
Save page as...			Ctrl+S
Find...			Ctrl+F
Print...			Ctrl+P
Zoom	−	100% +	⌐⌐
History			Ctrl+H
Downloads			Ctrl+J
Settings			
Report an issue...			
More tools			▶

1. Click the Customize and Control button in the Chrome browser and select Settings.

2. Go to the Search section and check the Enable Instant for Faster Searching option.

Search

Set which search engine is used when searching from the omnibox.

Google ▼ | Manage search engines... |

☑ Enable Instant for faster searching (omnibox input may be logged)

Use Google's Advanced Search

If you want to perform a more targeted search, you can use Google's Advanced Search page. You access the Advanced Search page by performing an initial search, clicking the Options (gear) button at the top of the search results page, and then clicking Advanced Search.

The Advanced Search page contains a number of options you can use to fine-tune your searches. All you have to do is make the appropriate selections on the page, and Google does all the fine-tuning for you.

```
Advanced Search

Find pages with...

all these words:              [ red car                                    ]

this exact word or phrase:    [                                            ]

any of these words:           [                                            ]

none of these words:          [                                            ]

numbers ranging from:         [                    ] to [                   ]

Then narrow your results
by...

language:                     [ any language                            ▼ ]

region:                       [ any region                              ▼ ]

last update:                  [ anytime                                 ▼ ]

site or domain:               [                                            ]
```

Advanced Search page

What options are available on the Advanced Search page? The following table provides the details.

Options on Google's Advanced Search Page

Option	Description
Find pages with **all these words**	Google's default search mode.
Find pages with **this exact word or phrase**	Searches for the exact phrase entered.
Find pages with **any of these words**	Searches for either one word or another, instead of for both words.
Show pages with **none of these words**	Excludes pages that contain specified word(s).
Show pages with **numbers ranging from**	Enables you to search for a range of numbers.
Narrow your results by **language**	Searches for pages written in a specific language.
Narrow your results by **region**	Narrows the search to a given country.
Narrow your results by **last update**	Lets you search for the most recent results—past 24 hours, past week, past month, past year, or anytime.
Narrow your results by **site or domain**	Restricts the search to the specified website or domain
Narrow your results by **terms appearing**	Restricts the search to certain areas of a page—title, text, URL, links to, or anywhere.
Narrow your results by **SafeSearch**	Filters mature content from the search results.
Narrow your results by **reading level**	Displays a graph of reading levels on the search results page; you can then click a reading level to show only those pages written at that level.
Narrow your results by **file type**	Limits the search to specific types of files.

Option	Description
Narrow your results by **usage rights**	Lets you search for pages based on whether the content is free to share in various ways—not filtered by license; free to use or share; free to use or share, even commercially; free to use, share, or modify; or free to use, share, or modify, even commercially.

Additional links at the bottom of the page enable you to find pages that are similar to a given page, search pages you've previously visited, use search operators in the search box, and customize your search settings.

Understand Search Results

After you enter your search query, Google searches its index for all the web pages that match your query. Then it displays the results on a search results page.

Interestingly, each results page is unique; what you see depends on what you're searching for. In fact, the same query made on different days, or by different users, might return different results. That's just Google's way of trying to serve the best results for each individual user.

That said, there are some common elements you're likely to encounter as a result of a Google Search. These include the following:

Search statistics   Search tools   Search box   Search button   Click to enable SafeSearch filtering

Google que books   Michael Miller 0 +

Web Images Maps Shopping More Search tools   SafeSearch

10 personal results. 197,000,000 other results.

Que: Computing & Technology Books, Video, Articles for Home ...
www.quepublishing.com/
Learn Office, Windows, Mac OS X, Facebook, Twitter, iPhone, iPad, and more with Que books, articles, web editions, eBooks, video, podcasts, blogs, ...

Books
1. Kodu for Kids: The Official Guide to Creating Your Own Video ...

Register your Product
Register a Product. Register the Que Publishing products you ...

About Us
The Que series of products are all about helping you learn about ...

Write for Us
Write for Us. Que Publishing, a publishing imprint of Pearson ...

Using Series
The USING series is more than just books; don't just read about it ...

Gadgets & Hardware
Gadgets & Hardware Resource Center from Que Publishing ...

More results from quepublishing.com »

Que Publishing | InformIT
www.informit.com/imprint/index.aspx?st=61090
Que Publishing is excited to announce our new web site, quepublishing.com. We gathered our consumer products in one easy place—look for **books**, eBooks, ...

Click to hide personal results   Options button

Page title   URL   Page excerpt

- **Search box**—This is where you can enter a new search query.

- **Search button**—Click here, after you've entered a new query, to initiate the search.

- **Search tools**—Click any of these options to display only web pages, images, maps, shopping results, and such. Click the Search Tools button to display additional filtering options for your specific search.

- **Search statistics**—This displays how many results were returned for your query, and how long it took to display those results. In some cases, this bar also includes a link to a definition of the keyword.

- **Ads**—These are paid ads by Google's advertisers. You should not confuse these ads with the "organic" search results, as they might have only indirect relevance to your query. These ads typically are positioned to the right of the main search results, and sometimes above the main results.

- **Page title**—For each search result, Google displays the title of the page. The title is a clickable link; click it to view the linked-to page.

- **URL**—This is the full web address of the selected web page. It is *not* a clickable link; you have to click the page title to jump to the page.

- **Page excerpt**—Below the page title is an excerpt from the associated web page. This may be the first few sentences of text on the page, a summary of page contents, or something similar.

Local Searches

If Google thinks you're looking for something locally, Google often displays a map on the right side of the search results page. Local businesses that match your query are pinpointed on the map; these businesses are displayed in the search results under a Places heading. Click the Places heading or the map to display a full page of local results, via Google Maps.

Change Search Providers

By default, Google Chrome uses Google for all of its browser-based searches. You can, however, change this so that you send all your queries to Yahoo! or Bing or to another search site of your choice.

1. Click the Customize and Control button and select Settings.

2. Go to the Search section and select a provider from the pull-down list: Google, Yahoo!, or Bing.

3. Click the Manage Search Engines button to choose from additional search providers.

4. Select from one of the choices in the Other Search Engines section, or enter a new search engine in the fields provided.

5. Click OK.

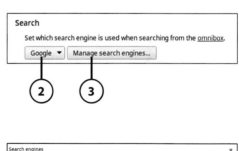

Managing Your Home Page

In a traditional web browser, the Home page is the page that opens when you first launch the browser. With the Google Chrome OS, the Home page is the one that appears when you first turn on your Chromebook—as well as when you click the Home button next to Chrome's Address box.

Choose a New Home Page

By default, Chrome displays its New Tab page as its Home page. You can, however, specify any web page as Chrome's Home. To do so, you need to know the URL of the page you want to go to.

1. Click the Customize and Control button and then select Settings.

2. Go to the Appearance section and check Show Home Button.

3. Click Change beside the New Tab Page item to display the Home Page panel.

4. Check Open This Page.

5. Enter the URL for the desired page.

6. Click OK.

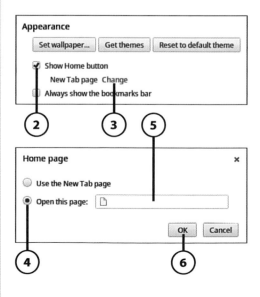

Display the Home Button

Chrome can display a Home button, next to the Address bar, that opens the Home page when clicked. This button is not displayed by default; you need to enable it.

1. Click the Customize and Control button and then select Settings.

2. Go to the Appearance section and check the Show Home Button option.

New tab			Ctrl+T
New window			Ctrl+N
New incognito window			Ctrl+Shift+N
Bookmarks			▶
Edit	Cut	Copy	Paste
Save page as...			Ctrl+S
Find...			Ctrl+F
Print...			Ctrl+P
Zoom	−	100% +	⌟⌞
History			Ctrl+H
Downloads			Ctrl+J
Settings			
Report an issue...			
More tools			▶

Appearance

Set wallpaper...   Get themes   Reset to default theme

☑ Show Home button

Bookmarking Favorite Pages

Google Chrome enables you to keep track of your favorite web pages via the use of *bookmarks*. You can bookmark the pages you want to return to in the future and display your bookmarks in a bookmarks bar that appears just below Chrome's Address bar.

Favorites

Google Chrome's bookmarks are the same as Internet Explorer's "Favorites."

Bookmark a Web Page

There are several ways to bookmark a web page. The following steps are for the fastest method.

1. Navigate to the web page you want to bookmark.

2. Click the Bookmark This Page (star) icon in the Address box.

3. Chrome now bookmarks the page and displays the Bookmark Added! information bubble. Edit the name of the bookmark, if you want.

4. Pull down the Folder list to determine where you want to save this bookmark.

5. Click the Done button to save the bookmark.

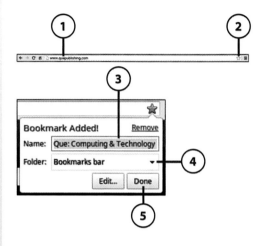

Display the Bookmarks Bar

To view your bookmarks, you need to display Chrome's Bookmarks bar. This is not turned on full-time; by default, it only appears at the top of the New Tab page.

You can, however, enable the Bookmarks bar so that it appears on every open tab. It displays beneath the Omnibox.

1. Click the Customize and Control button to display the drop-down menu.

2. Select Bookmarks, Show Bookmarks Bar.

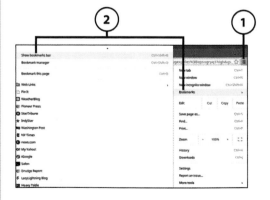

Go to a Bookmarked Page

With the Bookmarks bar visible, returning to a bookmarked page is as easy as clicking a button.

1. Click a button on the Bookmarks bar to display the bookmarked web page.

2. If you have more bookmarks than can fit in the width of the browser window, the bookmarks bar displays a double arrow on the far-right side. Click this double arrow to display the additional bookmarks in a drop-down menu.

Manage Bookmarks

Google Chrome enables you to organize your bookmarks into folders and subfolders that branch off from the bookmarks bar, as well as in other folders on the same level as the bookmarks bar. You do this by using Chrome's Bookmark Manager.

1. Click the Customize and Control button to display the drop-down menu.

2. Select Bookmarks, Bookmark Manager. In the Bookmark Manager that opens, the folders and subfolders of bookmarks are displayed in the left navigation pane; the individual bookmarks are displayed in the right pane.

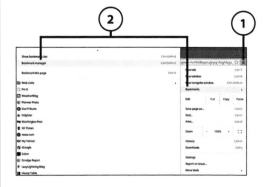

3. Select a folder or subfolder in the navigation pane to display the contents of that folder.

4. Click and drag a bookmark to a new position to change the order of bookmarks in a folder.

5. Select a folder, click the Organize button on the menu bar, and then select Reorder by Title to list a folder's bookmarks in alphabetical order.

6. Drag and drop a bookmark onto the new folder to move the bookmark to a different folder.

7. Click the Organize button and select Add Folder to create a new folder or subfolder.

8. To rename a folder, select that folder, click the Organize button, then select Rename and enter a new name for the folder.

9. To edit information about a specific bookmark, select the bookmark, click the Organize button, and then select Edit. You can then edit the bookmark's name and URL from within the URL list.

10. Select a bookmark, click the Organize button, and select Delete to remove the bookmark from the list.

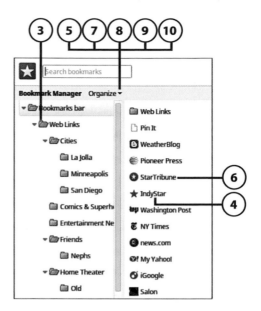

Browsing in Incognito Mode

Google Chrome, like most web browsers, keeps a record of every web page you visit. That's fine, but every now and then you might browse some web pages that you don't want tracked.

If you want or need to keep your browsing private, Google Chrome offers what it calls Incognito mode. In this special mode (actually, a separate browser window), the pages you visit aren't saved to your browser's history file, cookies aren't saved, and your activity is basically done without any record being kept.

Simultaneous Windows

Chrome enables you to run both normal and Incognito windows simultaneously.

Open an Incognito Window

1. Click the Customize and Control button to display the drop-down menu.

2. Click New Incognito Window.

3. A new Incognito window opens; it's recognizable by the little spy icon next to the first tab. You can switch between the Incognito and other open windows by pressing the Next Window button on your Chromebook's keyboard.

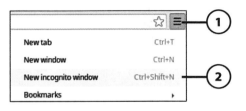

Chrome
Web Store

Search
for apps

Browse by
category

In this chapter, you discover how to add functionality to your Chromebook with Chrome apps and extensions.

→ Understanding Chrome Apps
→ Getting to Know the Chrome Web Store
→ Installing and Launching Apps
→ Managing Installed Apps
→ Examining Chrome Apps—by Category
→ Installing and Using Extensions

Using Chrome Apps and Extensions

If you have an iPhone or Android phone, you're used to the concept of *apps*—small, single-purpose applications that you run with the touch of a button. Well, there are apps available for your Chromebook, as well as a Chrome Web Store, to find the apps you want. In addition, the Chrome Web Store offers a number of useful *extensions* that plug right into the Chrome browser and add extra functionality to your online experience.

Understanding Chrome Apps

A Chrome app is, as the name implies, an application that you run in Google Chrome—a web-based application, to be precise. In fact, Chrome apps are actually advanced interactive websites; when you run an app, you access that website and the functionality offered there. The app runs entirely within the Chrome browser.

For example, the app called Google Calendar is a web-based calendar and scheduling application. You access the app from Google

Chrome, and it looks and acts like a regular application, but the app itself is hosted on Google's website, as is all your personal calendar and appointment data.

That said, Google ensures that Chrome apps look and act like the apps on your smartphone, and are always available to you, no matter what computer you're using. Find an app you like, and you can run it on your Chromebook as well as within the Chrome browser on a Windows or Mac PC.

Here's something else: Apps are always up to date. When you run an app, you're running the current version offered by that website. No time-consuming (or costly) updates or upgrades are necessary.

On your Chromebook, you easily access your apps by clicking Apps on the Launcher. This displays the Apps panel, which hosts 16 apps per page. Click the bars at the bottom of the pane to display the next page of apps, or use the Search box to search for a specific app. Click any app to launch it in a browser window or tab.

Apps pane

Apps icon

What kinds of Chrome apps are available? The list is long, and includes apps for listening to music, doing office work, editing photos, and even playing games. You can find a large selection of apps—most of them you can freely download—in the Google's Chrome Web Store.

Getting to Know the Chrome Web Store

The Chrome Web Store is an online marketplace, hosted by Google, where you can browse and download thousands of different apps, extensions, and themes for Google Chrome. To visit the Chrome Web Store, click the Web Store icon on Chrome's New Tab page, or go directly to chrome.google.com/webstore/.

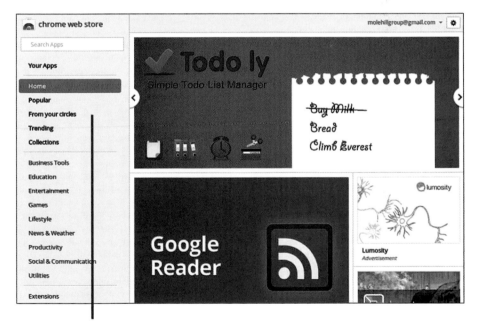

Browse the Chrome Web Store

Some of the items in the Chrome Web Store are developed by Google, others by various third-party developers. Most of these apps, extensions, and themes can run on any Chromebook; others can run on any Windows or Mac computer within the Chrome web browser.

Within the Chrome Web Store, you can browse for items by category, or search for items using the top-of-page search box. Each item in the Web Store has its own information page, where you can read more about the item, contribute your own rating and review, and download the item to your Chromebook.

Virtually all extensions and themes in the Chrome Web Store are free, as are most apps, but there are some apps that cost money to download. Other apps are free to download, but support in-app payments; that is, you might have to pay more in the future to continue using the app, or to activate enhanced functionality.

Installing and Launching Apps

As previously noted, you can find a large number of Chrome apps in the Chrome Web Store. Just open the Chrome browser and go to chrome.google. com/webstore/, or click Apps in the Launcher and then click Chrome Web Store.

Download and Install Apps

Chrome Apps are organized in the Chrome Web Store by cat-egory—Business Tools, Education, Entertainment, Games, Lifestyle, News & Weather, Productivity, Social & Communication, and Utilities. You can also display the most Popular apps, apps From Your Google+ Circle, Trending apps, and specific Collections of apps.

1. Click the Apps icon on the Launcher.

2. Click Chrome Web Store. The Chrome Web Store opens in the Chrome browser.

3. Click a category in the left sidebar to display a list of related subcategories; click the subcategory you want, and all the apps within the subcategory display.

4. By default, the apps are sorted by Recommended; click the Sort By list at the top of the page to instead sort by Popular, Trending, or Rating.

5. To learn more about a specific app, click it.

6. The Overview tab displays by default; click the Details tab to view more specifics, or the Reviews tab to see what others say about this app.

7. Click the Add to Chrome button at the top of the page to install the app.

8. Click the Add button to confirm the installation.

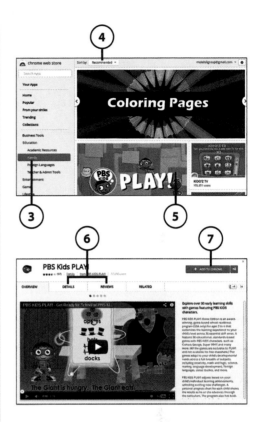

Launch Chrome Apps

After you install a Chrome app, it appears on the Apps pane that displays when you click Apps in the Chrome Launcher.

1. Click the Apps icon on the Launcher

2. Click the icon for the app you want to open.

Using Chrome Apps

Like traditional desktop applications, every Chrome app is different, and works in its own unique fashion. Creating a document in Google Docs, for example, is much different from reading posts in TweetDeck or playing Angry Birds. You'll need to get to know each app you install to learn its proper usage.

Managing Installed Apps

Chrome makes it easy to manage the apps you've installed. In fact, because an app is really just a link to a web page, there's really nothing concrete to uninstall—although you can configure how apps are launched

Configure App Options

Some Chrome apps have their own configuration options. For example, Google Docs lets you configure how items are opened and updated, among other settings. Those items with configuration options display an Options item when you right-click their icons in the Apps panel.

1. Click the Apps icon on the Launcher.

2. Right-click (two-finger tap) the item to configure and select Options.

3. When the options panel for that item opens, make the appropriate settings.

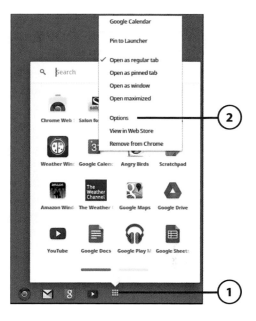

Uninstall Apps

If you find you're not using a given app, you can remove the link to that app from the Apps panel.

1. Click the Apps icon on the Launcher.

2. Right-click the item to delete and select Remove from Chrome.

3. When asked to confirm the uninstallation, click the Remove button.

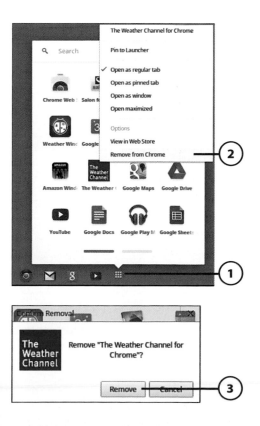

Determine How Apps Are Launched

By default, all Chrome apps open in a regular tab in the Chrome browser. You can change this launch behavior, however, and opt to have any given app open as follows:

- **Open as a regular tab**—This is the default option.

- **Open as a pinned tab**—This automatically opens a tab for the app whenever you start your Chromebook; the tab for the app is always there in the Chrome browser. (Pinned apps have smaller tabs than regular tabs, and always appear first on the row of tabs; plus, they can't be closed.)

- **Open as Window**—This opens a new window for the app when you launch it.

- **Open maximized**—This launches the app in full-screen mode—actually, as a normal tab but viewed full screen.

You can select launch options for any app installed on your Chromebook.

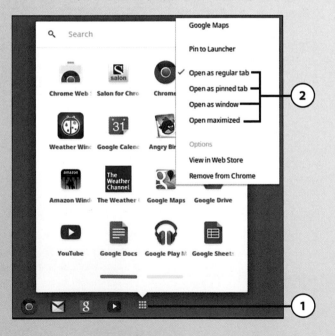

1. Click the Apps icon on the Launcher.

2. Right-click the item and select from one of the Open options.

Examining Chrome Apps—by Category

What kinds of Chrome apps are available? It's a comprehensive list, much like one of traditional software applications.

Business Tools

Google offers business-related apps in four major subcategories: Accounting & Finance; HR, Legal & Logistics; Marketing & Analytics; and Sales & CRM. Some of the more popular of these apps include the following:

HR and CRM

HR stands for human resources. CRM stands for customer relations management.

- **Cash Organizer**—Manage your personal and family finances.

- **Currency Converter**—Converts any currency to any other currency.

- **Financial Calculator**—Includes mortgage, loan term, loan amount, interest, and other calculators.

- **SEO SERP Workbench**—Monitor your website's search engine placements across multiple search engines.

- **Sprout Social**—Social media management tools.

- **W2MO**—Modeling, 3D simulation and animation, and workforce planning.

- **Zoho CRM**—Customer relations management.

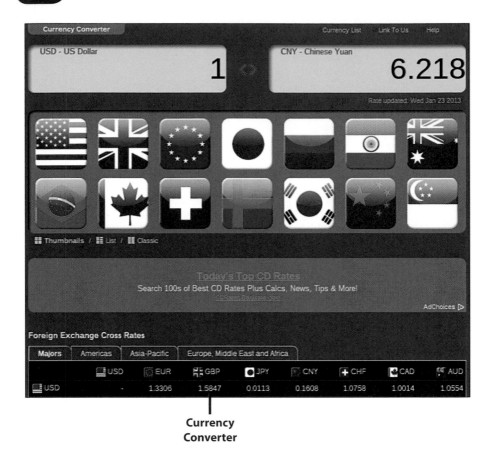

**Currency
Converter**

Education

The Chrome Apps Store offers a number of apps with educational value for students of all ages. The Education category is organized into four major subcategories: Academic Resources, Family, Foreign Languages, and Teacher & Admin Tools. Most, but not all, of these educational apps are free. The most popular include the following:

- **3D Solar System Web**—Explore the solar system with 3D models.

- **Biodigital Human**—Explore the body with 3D models.

- **Daum Equation Editor**—Online scientific equation creation and editing.

- **Kido'z TV**—Turns your browser into a safe viewing platform for your kids.

- **Learn French/Italian/Spanish/Portuguese/Hebrew/etc**—A series of popular language tutors.

- **Planetarium**—An interactive sky map for exploring stars and planets.

- **Thesaurus**—As the title says, an online thesaurus.

- **Typing Test** and **Type Fu**—Two popular typing tutors.

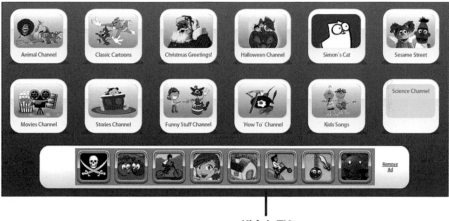

Kido'z TV

Entertainment Apps

Your Chromebook is actually a pretty decent little entertainment device—especially with the right apps installed. The Entertainment section in the Chrome Web Store is divided into the following major subcategories: Books, Music & Radio, Online Video, Photos, and TV & Movies. Here are some of the more popular apps in this section:

- **Audiotool**—A powerful online music production studio, for making your own kind of music.

- **BeFunky Photo Editor**—Photo editing and special effects.

- **Google Play Books**—Choose from more than 4 million books to read online.

- **Google Play Music**—Google's music storage/streaming service.

- **Internet TV**—Watch Internet TV from around the world, online.

- **Kindle Cloud Reader**—Read ebooks on your Chromebook from Amazon's Kindle store.

- **Marvel Comics**—Digital versions of poplar Marvel comic books, including Spider-Man, Iron Man, Thor, Captain America, and the X-Men.

- **Pandora**—Streaming music from one of the web's largest music libraries.

- **Picasa**—Access to Google's Picasa Web Albums.

- **PicMonkey**—Advanced photo editing.

- **Psykopaint**—Creates interesting art from existing digital photos.

- **Webcam Toy**—Take photos from your Chromebook's webcam and apply more than 70 fun effects.

- **YouTube**—A front end to Google's popular video sharing site.

BeFunky Photo Editor

Games

Let's face it; most people spend a lot of time playing games on their computers. Your Chromebook is no exception, which is why you can find lots of fun (and addictive) games in the Chrome Web Store, organized into the following subcategories: Arcade & Action, Board & Card, Puzzle & Brain, Role-Playing & Strategy, Sports Games, and Virtual Worlds.

The following are some of the most popular games in the Chrome Web Store:

- **Angry Birds**—Of course, today's most popular online game is available for Chrome. If you haven't played it yet, go ahead—everybody else is. (This game has more than 10 million users from the Chrome Web Store.)

- **Bejeweled**—Popular gem-swapping strategy game.

- **Cargo Bridge**—All about building bridges.

- **Contract Killer**—Popular shooter upper.

- **Crazy Rollercoaster**—Construct your own rollercoaster—and then ride it.

- **Cut the Rope**—An award-winning all-ages game.

- **Entanglement**—Physics-based game that challenges you to create the longest path possible.

- **Gun Bros**—A first-person shooter.

- **Isoball 3**—Challenging puzzle games.

- **Little Alchemy**—Create awesome things with selected elements.

- **Plants vs. Zombies**—Award-winning game that has you defending your home from zombies, using an arsenal of zombie-zapping plants.

- **Poppit**—A Tetris-like balloon popping game for all ages.

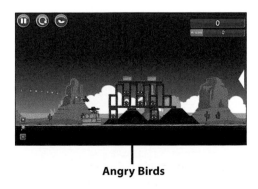

Angry Birds

Lifestyle Apps

The Chrome Web Store offers all sorts of apps that match your busy lifestyle, organized into the following categories: Astrology, Food & Health, Money, Religion, Shopping, and Travel. The most popular include the following:

- **BBC GoodFood**—A recipes app, with more than 260 healthy (and free) recipes.

- **Bible**—An online app for reading, listening to, and sharing the Bible.

- **eBay Web App**—Manage your eBay auctions from within Chrome.

- **Gojee**—Fashion and food reporting.

- **Google Finance**—Financial news, stock quotes, performance charts, and more.

- **Mint**—Web-based financial management.

- **Personal Trainer**—Exercises and workout routines.

- **TouristEye Planner**—Plan your trip online.

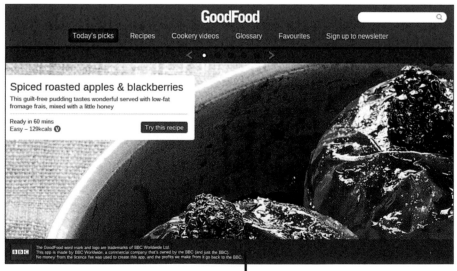

BBC GoodFood

News & Weather Apps

There's lots of news on the Web; use the apps in this category to find it. The Chrome Web Store offers apps in the following subcategories: News Reporting, Social News, Sports, and Weather Forecasts, the most popular of which include

- **Full Screen Weather**—More weather conditions and forecasts, from the Weather Underground.

- **Google News**—A front end to Google's online news headlines.

- **Google Reader**—Online RSS newsreader.

- **New York Times**—A specialized app for reading the *Times* within the Chrome browser.

- **The Weather Channel for Chrome**—Forecasts, radar, and current conditions for up to nine locations, from the folks at The Weather Channel.

- **Weather Window by WeatherBug**—A cool, graphical way to view current weather conditions—in a virtual window in your Chrome browser.

Weather Window by WeatherBug

Productivity Apps

As far as Google is concerned, productivity apps include Creative Tools, Developer Tools, Office Applications, Search & Browsing Tools, and Task Management. The most popular of these productivity apps include the following:

- **Audodesk Homestyler**—Plan your own home remodeling projects.

- **Dropbox**—Store and share your files online with this service that competes with Google Drive.

- **Google Calendar**—Another popular Google app, for keeping schedules and appointments.

- **Google Drive**—The front-end to Google's online file storage service.

- **Google Maps**—Online maps and directions.

- **Google Search**—A front-end to Google's online search engine.

- **Microsoft Hotmail**—Microsoft's popular web-based email service.

- **My Chrome Theme**—Create and share your own Google Chrome themes.

- **Pixlr-o-matic**—Convert your digital photos into cool-looking retro pics.

Google Maps

Social & Communication Apps

Social networking is a big deal; you never want to be away from your Twitter or Facebook feeds. To that end, Google offers apps in the following social and communication subcategories: Blogging, Chat & IM, Email & Contacts, Phone & SMS, and Social Networking.

Here are the most popular of these apps:

- **Gmail Offline**—Enables you to read and create Gmail email messages, even when your Chromebook isn't connected to the Internet.

- **Google+**—A front-end to Google's new social network.

- **imo messenger**—Chat with your friends on Skype, Facebook, Yahoo! Messenger, AIM, Google Talk, and other popular instant messaging services.

- **persona**—Enables you to read your Facebook and Twitter feeds in a single app.

- **TweetDeck**—From Twitter, a front-end to manage communications across multiple social networks.

- **WordPress**—Manage and post to your WordPress blogs.

TweetDeck

Utilities

Whatever we haven't yet covered probably falls into the Utilities category, and the following subcategories: Alarms & Clocks, Bookmarks, Calculators, Dictionaries, and Notepads. Here are some of the more popular utility apps in the Chrome Web Store:

- **Calculator**. Popular scientific calculator.

- **Digital Clock**—Customizable onscreen clock.

- **Evernote Web**—Award-winning note taking/sharing app.

- **Numerics Calculator & Converter**—Powerful Chrome-based calculator and converter.

- **QR Code Generator**—Create your own QR (quick reference) codes.

- **QuickNote**—Take notes from within the Chrome browser.

- **Springpad**—Create and share topic-focused notebooks.

- **Sticky Notes**—More onscreen notes for Chrome.

- **Stopwatch**—An easy-to-use online stopwatch.

- **World Clocks**—Interactive analog and digital clocks from more than 400 cities worldwide.

Calculator

Installing and Using Chrome Extensions

Google Chrome is an interesting operating system in that Google encourages outside developers to add increased functionality. This is done via the use of *extensions* that install within Chrome and enable you to perform specific tasks.

For example, you can add Chrome extensions to block web page ads, display how many unread messages you have in your Gmail inbox, view status updates on Facebook or Twitter, view dictionary definitions, and capture screenshots of web pages. There are thousands of these extensions available, and they're all free.

You can find Chrome extensions in the Chrome Web Store; just scroll down and click Extensions in the left sidebar. From there, you can use the top-of-page Search box to search for specific extensions by keyword, or browse available extensions.

Free Extensions
You can download all the extensions in the Chrome Web Store for free.

Download and Install Extensions

Extensions are organized in the Chrome Web Store by category—Accessibility, Blogging, By Google, Developer Tools, Fun, News & Weather, Photos, Productivity, Search Tools, Shopping, Social & Communication, and Sports. You download and install extensions the same way you do Chrome apps.

1. From within the Chrome Web Store, scroll down and click Extensions in the left sidebar.

2. Click a category to view extensions of that type.

3. Click an extension to learn more.

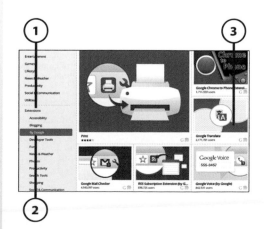

4. Read about the extension and then click the Add to Chrome button if you decide to install.

5. When asked to confirm the new extension, click the Add button.

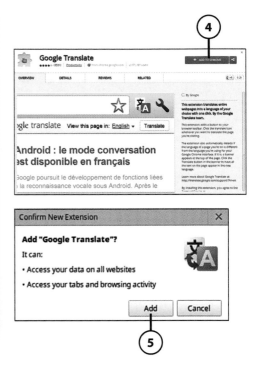

Use Extensions

How do you use Chrome extensions? It all depends; every extension is different, although many tend to install some sort of access button next to Chrome's Address box.

For example, the YoWindow Weather extension installs a new button next to the Chrome Omnibox; this button displays the current weather and temperature. When you click the YoWindow Weather button, the extension displays an information pane with your current weather conditions and forecast.

You also get a new button installed when you download the Cloudy Calculator extension. Click this button and you see a scrolling calculator window, with an input field at the bottom. Enter your equation into the input field, press Enter, and the Cloudy Calculator calculates the answer for you.

Obviously, other extensions work differently, but you get the picture. Add as many extensions as you like to add functionality to Chrome and your Chromebook.

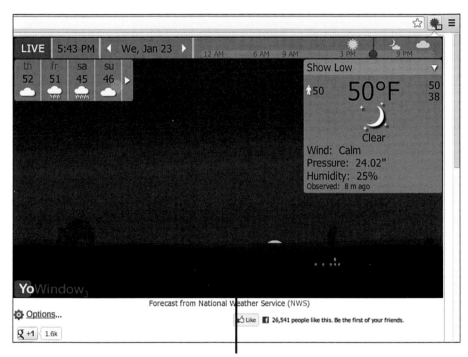

YoWindow Weather

Cloudy Calculator

Manage Chrome Extensions

Some extensions can be configured for your personal use. For example, weather-related extensions typically need your location information to display local conditions and forecasts. You can also opt to run a given extension in Chrome's Incognito anonymous browsing mode.

1. Open the Chrome browser and click the Customize and Control button to display the drop-down menu.

2. Select More Tools, Extensions to open a page that lists all the extensions you've downloaded.

3. Check the Allow in Incognito box if you want the extension to be available when browsing in Incognito mode.

4. If an extension has configurable options, it displays an Options link next to the Allow in Incognito item; click this link to configure the option. (Not all extensions have configurable options.)

5. Uncheck the Enabled box for an extension to disable it.

6. Click the Remove from Chrome (trashcan) icon for an extension to totally delete the extension from your Chromebook.

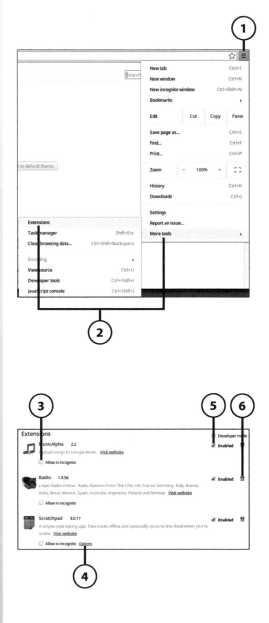

Enabling Disabled Extensions

You can later enable any extension you've disabled by returning to the Extensions page and clicking Enable for that extension. You cannot undelete a deleted extension; if you want it back, you need to reinstall it from the Chrome Web Store.

APPS VERSUS EXTENSIONS: WHICH IS WHICH?

>>>Go Further

Chrome extensions seem similar to Chrome apps in that they both offer some sort of added functionality not present in Chrome itself. In reality, they are much different.

A Chrome app is a freestanding web-based application that helps you perform a specific task. Apps exist on external websites, not within the browser. You run an app when you need to run it, and not before.

A Chrome extension, on the other hand, is a plug-in for the Chrome OS or Chrome browser that adds features and functionality. Extensions are installed within Chrome, and run automatically whenever Chrome is running.

So an app is something separate from Chrome, whereas an extension is something that runs within Chrome. In addition, apps tend to be larger in scope, and extensions tend to be very specific in the functionality offered.

In reality, you'll probably use both apps and extensions with your Chromebook. Extensions are great for adding little features to the OS, whereas apps are necessary for performing larger tasks, such as word processing or scheduling. You should check out some of both.

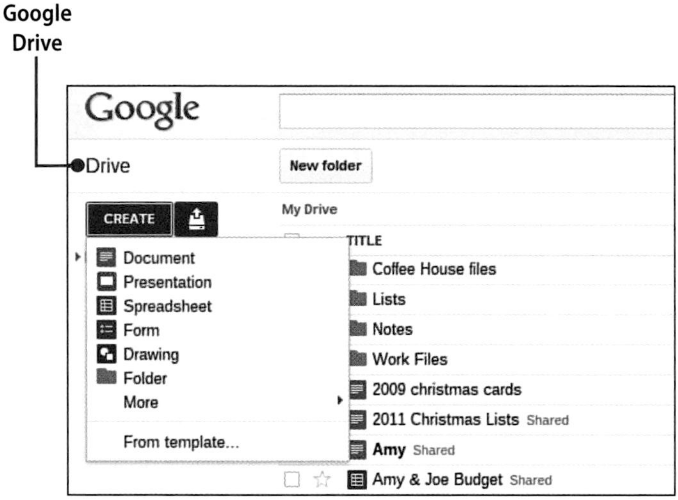

Google
Drive

Google

●Drive   New folder

CREATE 📤   My Drive
                        TITLE
▸ 📄 Document   📁 Coffee House files
  ▢ Presentation   📁 Lists
  📊 Spreadsheet   📁 Notes
  ☷ Form   📁 Work Files
  ◼ Drawing   ▸ 📄 2009 christmas cards
  📁 Folder   📄 2011 Christmas Lists Shared
     More   📄 Amy Shared
     From template... ▢ ☆ 📊 Amy & Joe Budget Shared

In this chapter, you learn about web-based alternatives to traditional desktop applications.

→ Office Suites in the Cloud
→ Word Processing in the Cloud
→ Spreadsheets in the Cloud
→ Presentations in the Cloud
→ Photo Editing in the Cloud
→ Calendars in the Cloud
→ Email in the Cloud

Working in the Cloud

If you're used to using a traditional Windows or Mac computer, you're probably used to using specific software programs. Well, none of those programs work on your new Chromebook; Chromebooks don't run any traditional software, if you recall.

So how do you do what you used to do now that you have a new Chromebook? It's all a matter of finding web-based alternatives to traditional software programs—of which there are many.

Office Suites in the Cloud

The most popular productivity software program today is Microsoft Office, with its combination of word processing (Word), spreadsheet (Excel), and presentation (PowerPoint) functionality. Since you probably use Office either at work or at home (or both), you need a web-based alternative to this traditional desktop software suite. There are several to choose from.

The most popular of these cloud productivity suites come from Google, Zoho, and—believe it or not—Microsoft. Of these suites,

Google Drive has the largest installed base today; many companies, organizations, and educational institutions have already switched from Microsoft Office to Google's free web-based applications. But don't rule out any of the competing suites, especially Microsoft's Office Web Apps and Office Live 365; the latter, despite its higher cost, will have enormous appeal to corporations currently running Office software.

Which of these suites is best for your own use? It depends on what you want. If compatibility with existing Microsoft Office software is your prime concern, you can't go wrong with Microsoft's Office Web Apps or Office 365. The former is free and good for basic editing; the latter costs money but provides more complete Office functionality. If collaboration is your focus, Google Drive can't be beat. In terms of ease of use, especially in file management, both Google Drive and Zoho Office do a great job. I'll also give Google Drive the lead in speed; it's a pretty zippy suite of apps, compared to the competition.

Bottom line, if you're looking for office productivity online, you need to check out all the major players. There are pluses and minuses to each, but you're sure to find one that best suits the way you like to work.

Google Drive

Google Drive (drive.google.com) is not only Google's online storage service, it's also a web-based office suite. As you might suspect, Google Drive (formerly known as Google Docs) works very well with Google's Chrome OS and Chromebooks. It also integrates seamlessly with Google's other apps and services; if you choose Google, you get kind of a one-stop-shop for all your Chromebook computing needs.

The Google Drive suite contains three separate applications, which are covered in more depth later in this chapter:

- Docs (word processor)

- Sheets (spreadsheets)

- Slides (presentations)

Google Drive ———

Forms and Drawing
Google Drive also includes Forms and Drawing apps, but those aren't really traditional office applications.

File management for all three apps is integrated into your Google Drive account. When you access your Google Drive from Chrome's File Manager, you see all your word processing, spreadsheet, and presentation files in one place. For full functionality, you have to log onto Google Drive (drive.google. com) from the Chrome browser; from this web-based Google Drive dashboard, you can create new documents, open existing ones, and even import documents from Microsoft Word, Excel, and PowerPoint. The Google Drive web dashboard looks a little like the Gmail inbox, and works pretty much the same way.

It's Not All Good

Office Compatibility

Although Google Drive claims file compatibility with Microsoft Office, you need to take that with a grain of salt. Google Drive can import Word, Excel, and PowerPoint files (and export back to those formats), but not all formatting survives the translation. If you have a document with a lot of fancy formatting, expect some of that formatting to be lost when you import into Google Drive. In addition, because Google Drive apps don't have all the functionality of their Microsoft Office competitors, some functionality might be lost when importing.

Google Drive is probably the best of all web-based suites for sharing and collaboration. Online file sharing is one of Google's overall strengths, of course; if you plan on collaborating online on group projects, Google Drive is the way to go.

Another big advantage of the Google Drive suite is that it's free. There's no one-time fee or ongoing subscription fee; you log on with your Google Account and you're ready to go.

Google Apps

Although Google Drive is free for individuals to use, Google does offer a paid version of the suite, dubbed Google Apps, designed specifically for corporations and other large institutions. This paid version is essentially the same as the free Google Drive, but with enhanced storage and support for information technology (IT) departments. (There's also a version of Google Apps for Education, which many colleges use.)

Microsoft Office Web Apps

When Google jumped out into an early lead in the market for web-based productivity suites, you couldn't expect Microsoft to stand by idle. It took a little time, but Microsoft eventually came out with a web-based version of Microsoft Office, dubbed Office Web Apps. This cloud productivity suite includes web-based versions of the primary Office apps:

- Microsoft Word Online (word processing)

- Microsoft Excel Online (spreadsheets)

- Microsoft PowerPoint Online (presentations)

- Microsoft OneNote Online (note-gathering and information sharing)

If you need full compatibility with your existing Office documents then Office Web Apps is your web-based productivity suite of choice. A Word document is a Word document is a Word document, whether you're editing in the software-based version of Word or the online version of the app. Conversion errors are few and far between.

In addition, Office Web Apps contain much of the same functionality as the software version of Microsoft Office. (Most, but not all; some sacrifices have been made for online use.) Still, it's a fairly seamless transition from Microsoft Office software to Office Web Apps.

The consumer version of Office Web Apps is part of Microsoft's SkyDrive cloud-based storage solution, located at office.microsoft.com/web-apps/. It's free for consumer use.

Microsoft Office 365

Microsoft Office Web Apps are also available to small and medium-sized businesses via the Office 365 service. Office 365 consists of the three basic Office apps plus additional applications:

- Microsoft Word Online
- Microsoft Excel Online
- Microsoft PowerPoint Online
- Microsoft OneNote Online
- Microsoft Outlook Online (email/scheduling)
- Microsoft Publisher Online (desktop publishing)
- Microsoft Access Online (database management)
- Microsoft InfoPath Online (form design/management)
- Microsoft Exchange Online (messaging/personal information management)
- Microsoft SharePoint Online (collaboration and sharing)
- Microsoft Lync Online (instant messaging and web conferencing)

Microsoft also offers a Home Premium version of Office 365, available for a $99.99 per-year subscription. This version includes the Word, Excel, PowerPoint, Outlook, OneNote, Access, and Publisher online apps. If you absolutely, positively need to use the full version of Office, it's worth considering—even if it's on the pricey side. Learn more at www.microsoft.com/office365/.

Zoho Docs

The other major player in web-based productivity suites is Zoho Docs. Zoho's individual word processing, spreadsheet, and presentation offerings are every bit the equal of those in Google Drive. Also like Google Drive, Zoho features impressive sharing and collaboration features, including a proprietary instant chat feature.

Zoho Docs includes the following applications:

- Zoho Writer (word processing)

- Zoho Sheets (spreadsheets)

- Zoho Show (presentations)

Zoho was one of the first companies in the web-based application space. As such, the company claims a fairly large and loyal user base, with more than 4 million users of its web-based applications.

Zoho Docs is free for personal use. Business users might need to sign up for Zoho's subscription versions, which runs $3 to $5 per month per user. (Volume discounts are available.) Learn more at www.zoho.com/docs/.

Word Processing in the Cloud

Big productivity suites aside, let's look a bit at the individual apps available, starting with word processing. Just about everyone who uses a computer uses a word processing program—most likely, some version of Microsoft Word. People use Word to do almost any type of writing, from memos and thank-you notes to big reports and newsletters.

You need to find some alternative to Word, then, if you want to be productive with your Chromebook. Not surprisingly, the top three cloud word processing apps come from Google, Microsoft, and Zoho.

Google Docs

Google Docs (drive.google.com) is the most popular web-based word processor available today. Like all things Google, the Google Docs interface is clean and, most important, it works well without imposing a steep learning curve. Basic formatting is easy enough to do, storage space for your documents is generous, and sharing/collaboration version control are a snap to do.

The Docs word processor looks a lot like Microsoft Word—or at least an older version of Word, before it went to the "ribbon" interface. You have a big blank space to create your document, a pull-down menu bar, and a toolbar with common commands. It's pretty familiar looking and fairly easy to use.

That said, Google Docs doesn't include all the functionality you're used to in Microsoft Word. In particular, Docs lacks some of Word's more sophisticated document formatting. But Google Docs is a decent replacement for Word if your needs are fairly traditional; it should do for the majority of everyday users. And, like all Google apps, Google Docs is free.

Microsoft Word Web App

The web-based version of Microsoft Word is the Word Web App (office.microsoft.com/web-apps/). The Word Web App looks and feels pretty much like the desktop version of Word, which shouldn't be surprising.

Obviously, the Word Web App is the app of choice if you want to maintain full compatibility with desktop versions of Word. It's also free for personal use; businesses should look into a subscription to Office Live 365, which includes the Word Web App.

Zoho Writer

As previously noted, Zoho's web-based applications are right up there with Google in terms of functionality and features, and this is especially true of Zoho Writer. This app easily holds its own against, if not surpasses, Google Drive in the web-based word processor race.

Zoho Writer (www.zoho.com/docs/) displays multiple documents in a single window, thanks to the app's tabbed interface. You get all the standard editing and formatting features, as well as page numbering, headers and footers, footnotes and endnotes, tables of contents, and other advanced features not found in all other web-based word processors.

Like Google Drive, Zoho Writer is a free application.

Spreadsheets in the Cloud

If the word processor is the most-used office application, then the spreadsheet is the second most-important app. Office users and home users alike use spreadsheets to prepare budgets, create expense reports, perform "what if?" analyses, and otherwise crunch their numbers.

There are several web-based spreadsheet applications that are worthy competitors to Microsoft's Excel software. As with word processors, the big three spreadsheet apps come from Google, Microsoft, and Zoho.

Google Sheets

Google Sheets (formerly known as Google Spreadsheets) was Google's first application in the Google Drive suite. (It's also the only app in the suite that Google developed in-house.) As befits its longevity, Google Sheets is Google's most sophisticated web-based application.

You access Google Sheets from the main Google Drive dashboard (drive.google.com). The Sheets workspace looks a lot like every other PC-based spreadsheet application you've ever used, whether you started with VisiCalc, 1-2-3, Quattro Pro, or Excel. You'll quickly recognize the familiar row-and-column grid; sure, the buttons or links for some specific operations might be in slightly different locations, but pretty much everything you expect to find is somewhere on the page.

In daily use, you'll find that Google Sheets is one of the most fully featured web-based spreadsheet applications available today, matching Excel almost feature to feature. It includes all the big features, including formulas and functions, charts, and even pivot tables. It's a worthwhile alternative to the Excel program—and it's completely free.

Microsoft Excel Web App

Of course, when it comes to alternatives to Microsoft Excel software, you definitely have to consider Microsoft's Excel Web App (office.microsoft.com/web-apps/). This app is essentially Excel on the Web, with many (but not all) of the same features available. As you might suspect, it looks and feels much like the desktop version of Excel; there's full file compatibility, as well.

Like other Office Web Apps, the Excel Web App is free for personal use; businesses should look into a subscription to Office Live 365, which includes the Word Web App.

Zoho Sheet

Zoho Sheet (www.zoho.com/docs/) is Zoho's web-based spreadsheet application. Like all Zoho apps, this one is fully featured with great sharing and collaboration features.

You get an Excel-like toolbar-based interface, multiple sheets in each file, a full load of functions, lots of different types of graphs, and all the formatting options you need to create great-looking printouts. Just as useful, Zoho Sheet lets you publish your web spreadsheets to your own website or blog; it's a simple one-button operation.

In short, Zoho Sheets is a leader in terms of features and functionality. It's definitely worth considering—especially at the price. (It's free.)

Presentations in the Cloud

One of the last components of the traditional office suite to move into the cloud is the presentation application. Microsoft PowerPoint has ruled the desktop forever, and it's proven difficult to offer competitive functionality in a web-based application; if nothing else, slides with large graphics are slow to access online in an efficient manner.

That said, there is a new crop of web-based presentation applications that aim to give PowerPoint a run for its money. The big players, as might be expected, are Google, Microsoft, and Zoho, but there are several other applications that are worth considering if you need to take your presentations with you on the road—or collaborate with users in other locations.

Google Slides

Google Slides, formerly known as Google Presentations, is the latest addition to the Google Drive suite of apps. It's meant to compete with Microsoft PowerPoint—although it lacks some of that program's features and functionality.

New and existing presentations are created and accessed from the main Google Drive dashboard (drive.google.com). The Sheets interface looks a lot like pre-2007 versions of PowerPoint, but with a few things missing. In particular, although you can include text, images, and shapes on a slide, there's no chart-making facility.

What you do get is the ability to add title, text, and blank slides; a PowerPoint-like slide sorter pane; a selection of predesigned themes; the ability to publish your file to the Web or export as a PowerPoint PPT or Adobe PDF file; and quick and easy sharing and collaboration, the same as with Google's other web-based apps.

If you use the other Google Drive apps, Sheets should be a natural choice. However, the lack of advanced presentation features might cause power PowerPoint users to look elsewhere for their online presentation needs.

Microsoft PowerPoint Web App

Desktop PowerPoint users will be right at home with Microsoft's PowerPoint Web App. That said, it suffers from some of the same limitations as do other web-based presentation apps—no slide transitions, no tables, no charts, and so forth. So although PowerPoint Web App looks and feels like the desktop version of PowerPoint, it's functionality is much less than what even casual users are used to.

You do get fairly good compatibility with regular PowerPoint files, though, limited functionality excepted. And it's free—at least to personal users. (Businesses should consider subscribing to Office Live 365 instead.)

Zoho Show

Zoho Show (www.zoho.com/docs/) is probably the weakest link in the Zoho Office suite. Like Google Presentations, Zoho Office enables you to create good-looking text-based slides, but that's about all. As with competing presentation apps, there is no charting function, no tables, and no slide transition effects.

That said, Zoho Show integrates well with Zoho's other web-based applications, and offers easy sharing and collaboration. So if you want a good basic presentation with few bells or whistles, it's worth checking out.

Other Presentation Apps

Presentations is one area where the big three don't have as big a lead as they do in other types of apps. That means you might want to check out some of the other popular web-based presentation apps, including Empressr (www. empressr.com) and SlideRocket (www.sliderocket.com).

Photo Editing in the Cloud

If you take a lot of pictures with your digital camera, you're used to touching up those photos with Adobe Photoshop Elements or some similar photo editing program. Obviously, you can't install a photo editing program on your Chromebook; instead, you have to do your photo editing online.

What can you do with an web-based photo editing app? Although you don't have quite the number of options you do with most desktop photo editing software, you do get all the basics. You can crop and rotate your photos, color correct them, fix the red eye effect, adjust contrast and brightness, and maybe even combine multiple photos into a photo collage.

Most of these cloud applications work by having you first upload your photo to the editing site. You then apply the edits you want, often by clicking a "quick fix" button of some sort. Your edited photo is then downloaded back to your Chromebook (or to your Chromebook's external storage) for archiving.

Adobe Photoshop Express Editor

This first web-based photo editing application is also arguably the best. Adobe Photoshop Express Editor (www.photoshop.com/tools/expresseditor/) certainly has a stellar lineage, coming from the same company that brings you Photoshop CS, the number-one photo editing program for serious photographers. As the name implies, Photoshop Express Editor is kind of a quick and dirty version of the full-featured Photoshop CS, with all the basic editing controls you need to fix the most common photo problems. And, best of all, it's completely free to use.

Photoshop Express Editor offers far and away the largest collection of editing/enhancement options of any online photo editor. Suffice to say, just about anything that's wrong with a photo, you can fix online with Photoshop Express.

Adobe lets you store up to 2GB of photos at any time. And, like many other web-based photo editors, Photoshop Express Editor is integrated with Flickr, so you can upload your edited photos to the Flickr site with a minimum of fuss and muss.

Other Online Photo Editors

Although Adobe's Photoshop Express Editor is an impressive (and free) service, there are several other free online photo editors worth checking out. These include the following:

- FotoFlexer (www.fotoflexer.com)

- PicMonkey (www.picmonkey.com)

- Picture2Life (www.picture2life.com)

- Pixlr (www.pixlr.com)

Finances and Banking in the Cloud

Users seem to be of two minds when it comes to handling their personal finances. Either you use your bank's website to handle all your transactions, or you use a financial program like Quicken.

If you're of the former persuasion, nothing changes with your Chromebook. You should still be able to access your bank's website and do all your banking from there.

If you're a Quicken user, however, you need to change the way you do things, as there's no web-based version of that traditional desktop program. That means you need to switch to using your bank's website, or go with Mint (www.mint.com), the leading web-based financial management program.

Actually, moving to Mint shouldn't be too tough for Quicken users, as they're both owned by the same company (Intuit). Unlike the increasingly expensive Quicken program, Mint is a free app, and works in much the same fashion. Although I'd never call moving all your financial information from one platform to another a simple process, this is probably as easy as it gets.

QuickBooks

If you run your own business, you probably use QuickBooks for your accounting needs. Fortunately, Intuit has an online version of QuickBooks that offers much of the same functionality as the desktop version. Learn more at quickbooks online.intuit.com.

Calendars in the Cloud

Most computer users today have embraced keeping their schedules on their PCs. Not that the old-fashioned wall-hanging calendar is dead, it's just that it's a whole lot easier to track appointments and events electronically; the computer does all the busywork for you.

It's even better when you use a cloud calendar app. A web-based calendar service stores your calendars on the Internet, where they can be accessed from any computer that has an Internet connection. This lets you check your schedule when you're on the road, even if your assistant in the office or your spouse at home has added new appointments since you left. Web-based calendars are also extremely easy to share with other users in any location, which make them great for collaborative projects.

Google Calendar

The most popular web-based calendar today, no doubt due to its association with the Web's most-used search engine, is Google Calendar (calendar. google.com). Google Calendar is free, full-featured, and easy to use. It lets you create both personal and shared calendars, which makes it ideal for tracking business group, family, and community schedules.

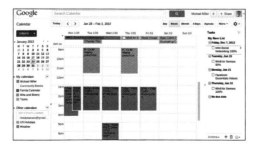

Google Calendar looks pretty much like every other calendar you've ever seen. You enter your appointments (which Google calls "events") directly into the calendar, which you can display in either daily, weekly, or monthly views. You can also, if you like, view your weekly agenda on a single page.

Because Google Calendar is web-based, you can use it to create not only a private calendar for yourself, but also public calendars for your company or organization. Create a public calendar and all employees or attendees can access it via the Web. In addition, special event invitation features make it easy to invite others to an event—public or private.

>>>Go Further

GOOGLE CALENDAR AND GMAIL

Here's something unique about Google Calendar. Because it's part of the mighty Google empire, Google Calendar integrates smoothly with Google's Gmail application. Google Calendar can scan your email messages for dates and times and, with a few clicks of your mouse, create events based on the content of your Gmail messages.

When you're reading a Gmail message that contains information pertaining to a possible event, just pull down the More Action menu and select Create Event. This opens a New Event window; enter the appropriate information, click Save Changes, and the event will be added to your Google Calendar.

Other Online Calendars

Most online calendars function similarly to Google Calendar, letting you schedule meetings and appointments, and often tracking tasks in to-do lists, too. Some popular alternatives include the following:

- Cozi Family Organizer (www.cozi.com)

- Hotmail Calendar (calendar.live.com)

- Yahoo! Calendar (calendar.yahoo.com)

- Zoho Calendar (www.zoho.com/calendar/)

Email in the Cloud

Traditional email is anything but cloud-based. The type of email program installed on most Windows and Mac computers uses a protocol called the Post Office Protocol (POP). POP email requires the use of a dedicated email *client* program, such as Microsoft Outlook, and—at the Internet Service Provider (ISP) level—separate email servers to send and receive messages.

Fortunately, there are cloud alternatives, in the form of web-based email services, also known as web mail or HTTP email. Unlike POP email, web mail can be accessed from any computer (including your Chromebook) using any web browser, and all your messages are stored on the Web, not locally. This lets you retrieve and manage your email when you're out of the office or on the road.

The three largest web mail services today are hosted by Google, Microsoft, and Yahoo!

Gmail

Google's web mail service is called Gmail (mail.google.com). Like most other web mail services, Gmail is completely web-based, works great with your Chromebook, and can be accessed from any computer or device with an Internet connection.

Also like the other services discussed in this chapter, Gmail is a free service; all you have to do is sign up for an account. Of course, if you already have a Google Account, that account can serve as your Gmail account. After you sign up for your Gmail account, you get assigned your email address (in the form of *name*@gmail.com) and you get access to the Gmail inbox page. And, of course, there's quick access to Gmail from your Chromebook, using the Gmail app.

Outlook.com

Hotmail was one of the first web-based email services, and it's still one of the largest. But it's not called "Hotmail" anymore; Microsoft has spruced it up, added new functionality, and renamed it as Outlook.com (www.outlook.com).

Like most web mail services, Outlook.com can be accessed from your Chromebook or any PC with a web browser and Internet connection. It's free to use.

Yahoo! Mail

Yahoo! Mail (mail.yahoo.com) is another web mail service, provided by the popular Yahoo! search site. The basic Yahoo! Mail is free, although Yahoo! also offers a paid service, Yahoo! Mail Plus, that lets you send larger messages if you like. The free version is fine for most users.

Yahoo! Mail gives you unlimited storage—which means you can effectively use Yahoo! Mail as an online backup or file storage system. All you have to do is email yourself those files you want to store and then place those messages (with attachments) in your designated storage folder.

In this chapter, you find out how to use Google Cloud Print to print documents from your Chromebook.

Printing with Google Cloud Print

Printing from Chrome OS is substantially different from printing from Microsoft Windows or the Mac OS. It's more like printing from an iPad or other tablet—you can't.

That's because like iOS and other tablet operating systems, Chrome OS doesn't have a native printing function. Instead, it uses a new service, called Google Cloud Print, to print over the Internet to supported printers.

This means that your printing choices might be somewhat limited; you need a printer that's compatible with Google Cloud Print, or access to a normal printer connected to Windows or Mac PC. Once everything's set up, printing is as simple as clicking a "print" button—only the setup is different.

Understanding Google Cloud Print

One of the things that makes Chrome OS different from other computer operating systems is that it doesn't carry with it a lot of legacy overhead—that is, the need to support older devices. That's one of the problems with Windows, for example; a large amount of programming code, disk space, and memory space is used to support thousands of printers and other devices from years past.

It's a necessary evil for those operating systems, however. If Windows or the Mac dropped support for all printers over a certain age, Microsoft and Apple would get a ton of angry calls and hate mail from users who had been abandoned. It's a real challenge, trying to add new features and keep a lean and mean OS while still supporting millions of users from the past two decades.

Google doesn't have that problem with Chrome OS; as a brand-new operating system; there are no users of older systems to support. But there is the challenge of making sure that Chrome is compatible with the hundreds and thousands of *current* devices used today. It's just as big an issue.

That is, it's only a big issue if you think that it's the operating system's job to directly interface with all these devices. Google obviously doesn't think so, and did *not* build in any native printing facility into Chrome OS. That is, Chrome OS doesn't include hundreds of different printer drivers, necessary to facilitate printing to different makes and models of printers. To Google, printer drivers are so old school; it's a Windows way of doing things.

Instead, Google has embraced a new technology dubbed Google Cloud Print. With this technology, Chrome is compatible with just a single device driver that's associated with the Cloud Print service. It's this service that connects to various printers, reducing the load on the operating system.

The way Google Cloud Print works is simple. When you launch the "print" function in Chrome, the OS sends the print command over the Internet to the designated Cloud Print printer. The printer isn't physically connected to your Chromebook; the entire process is web-based.

**HP Photosmart
Cloud Print printer**

Of course, you now have the issue of finding an Internet-ready printer that's compatible with Google Cloud Print. Some are, but many aren't. You need a printer that can connect wirelessly to your network or the Internet and can connect to the Cloud Print service, such as those in HP's ePrint line. Configuring one of these printers to work with Google Cloud Print and your Chromebook is a relatively easy operation.

But what do you do if you have a printer without built-in Cloud Print capability? Here Google relies on other computers in your household or business. Cloud Print can print to any existing printer, as long as it's connected to a Windows or Mac computer that has Internet access. That is, Cloud Print relies on the PC for the connection—which means you have to have a Windows or Mac computer handy (and powered up).

The nice thing about Google Cloud Print is that you can use it to print from just about any device. Yes, you can print from your Chromebook to a Cloud Print printer, but you can also print from your iPhone or Android smartphone, as well as from a Windows or Mac computer. And you can print from any location to any configured Cloud Print printer—which means you can be sitting in a hotel room in New York City and print to your Cloud Print printer back home in Omaha. No cables or printer drivers are necessary.

Connecting a Printer to Google Cloud Print

Before you can print from Google Chrome, you first must connect your printer to the Google Cloud Print service. You can connect either a Cloud Print-ready printer or an existing printers already connected to a Windows or Mac computer.

Connect a Cloud Print-Ready Printer

If you're looking for a Cloud Print-ready printer, models are available from Canon, Epson, HP, and Kodak. To use one of these printers for cloud printing, you must register it with the Google Cloud Print service. Follow your manufacturer's instructions to do so. (It's typically as simple as going to a registration page on the Web and entering your printer's email address.)

Connect a Non-Cloud Print-Ready Printer

To connect a printer that does not have built-in Cloud Print capability to the Google Cloud Print service, it must be connected to a Windows or Mac computer that is connected to the Internet. The computer must also be running the Google Chrome web browser. You then enable the Google Cloud Print Connector, which connects this computer's printers to the Cloud Print service.

1. On your Windows or Mac computer, open the Google Chrome browser and, if necessary, sign into your Google Account.

2. In the Chrome browser, click the Customize and Control button to display the drop-down menu.

3. Click Settings.

4. When the Settings page appears, scroll to the bottom of the page and click Show Advanced Settings. Go to the Google Cloud Print section and click the Add Printers button.

Google Cloud Print

Google Cloud Print lets you access this computer's printers from anywhere. Click to enable.

Add printers

④

5. When the Printer Confirmation page appears, click the Add Printer(s) button. This adds all printers currently connected to this PC to the Cloud Print service.

Google cloud print
beta

Printer confirmation

Click below to add all of the printers connected to this computer to Google Cloud Print for account molehillgroup@gmail.com.

This step is not required to print to Google Cloud Print. Clicking "Add printer(s)" will just add your local printers to your account. Cloud Ready Printers can connect directly without this step.

Add printer(s)

⑤

Disconnect a Printer from Cloud Print

You can, at any time, remove a printer from the Google Cloud Print service.

1. From within Chrome, go to https://www.google.com/cloudprint/manage.html.

2. Click the Printers tab.

3. Click the printer you want to disconnect.

4. Click the Delete button.

② ④ ③

Cloud Print (beta)   Delete   Share   Show Print Jobs   Rename   ↻   1–16 of 11 < >

Print Jobs   Brother MFC-7840W Printer   Owned by me
Printers   HP Deskjet Q2405 series   Owned by me

Google Cloud Print Home   Brother PC-FAX v.3.1   Owned by me
Add a Cloud-Ready Printer   Fax   Owned by me
Add a Classic Printer   Microsoft XPS Document Writer   Owned by me
    PaperPort Image Printer   Owned by me
    Print to FedEx Office
    QuickBooks PDF Converter   Owned by me
    Quicken PDF Printer   Owned by me
    Save to Google Drive

Printing to Google Cloud Print

After you've registered a printer with the Google Cloud Print service, printing from your Chromebook is as easy as clicking a button. In fact, you can print from any computer, smartphone, or other device to that printer; all you need to do is provide your Google Account information.

Print from Your Chromebook

To print from your Chromebook to a printer connected to Google Cloud Print, that printer must be powered on and connected to the Internet. If it's a "classic" printer, it must also be connected to a Windows or Mac PC that is connected to the Internet.

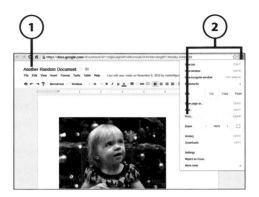

1. From within Chrome, open the web page or application document you want to print.

2. Press Ctrl+P, or click the Customize and Control button and select Print.

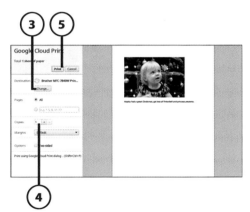

3. Go to the Destination section of the Google Cloud Print panel and click the Change button to select the printer you want to use.

4. Enter a number into the Copies box to print more than one copy.

5. Click the Print button.

Sharing a Printer

After you've registered a printer with the Google Cloud Print service, you can then opt to let other users share that printer. You can share a Cloud Print printer with any user who has a Google Account.

Share a Printer

To share a printer with another user, you have to tell Google Cloud Print that the user has permission to print.

1. From within Chrome, go to https://www.google.com/cloud-print/manage.html.

2. Click the Printers tab.

3. Click the printer you want to share.

4. Click the Share button to display the Sharing Settings dialog box.

5. Enter the email address or user-name of the person you want to share with into the large box at the bottom.

6. Click the Share button.

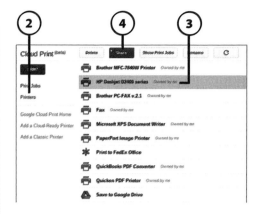

Disable Sharing

If, at a later date, you decide you no longer want to share your printer with a particular user, you can delete that person from your approved sharing list.

1. From within Chrome, go to https://www.google.com/cloudprint/manage.html.

2. Click the Printers tab.

3. Click the printer you want to not share.

4. Click the Share button to display the Sharing Settings dialog box.

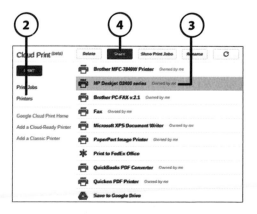

5. Go to the Permissions list and click the X next to that person's name.

6. Click the Close button.

5

HP Deskjet D2400 series sharing settings

Who has access:

🔒	Private		Change...
👤	Michael Miller (molehillgroup@gmail.com)		Owner
👤	Lew Archer (LewArcher2010@gmail.com)		Can print	×

Share   Close

6

Warning about
possible phishing
website

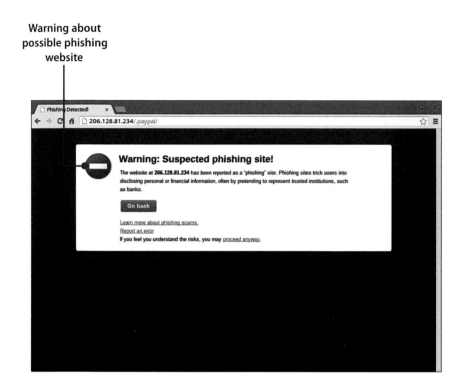

In this chapter, you find out why Chromebooks are more safe and secure than traditional computers—and how to make them even safer.

14

→ Cloud Computing and Data Security

→ Chrome OS and Malware

→ Protecting Against Phishing

→ Practicing Safe Computing

→ Configuring Chrome's Privacy and Security Settings

Using Google Chrome Safely and Securely

Many users are embracing Chromebooks because of security issues. That is, using a Chromebook with web-based storage is safer and more secure than using a traditional PC with local storage. You don't have to worry about computer viruses, spyware, and such; you don't even have to worry about someone hacking into your computer and stealing your data.

This security inherent in the Chrome model is great, but there are things you can do to make your Chromebook even more safe and secure. It's a matter of practicing safe computing—and knowing all your options.

Cloud Computing and Data Security

With Chrome OS, all your data is stored in the cloud; nothing is stored on your Chromebook. That makes for a uniquely secure computer system.

Unlike traditional desktop computing, where a hard disk crash can destroy all your valuable data, if your Chromebook crashes, it doesn't affect the storage of your data; all your data is still out there in the cloud, still accessible. In a world where few personal computer users back up their data on a regular basis, cloud computing is the ultimate in data-safe computing.

With cloud computing, all the important stuff is in the cloud, not on your computer. For example, it really doesn't matter if someone steals your Chromebook. (Other than the inconvenience, that is.) All a thief would get is a piece of hardware, but no personal data; that data remains in the cloud, accessible only by you, but from any computer.

Corporate information technology (IT) departments love this degree of data security. Cloud data is less likely to be stolen than data on a computer's hard drive. Because most Chromebooks don't even have a hard drive, what's to steal?

>>>Go Further

HOW SECURE IS YOUR DATA IN THE CLOUD?

With cloud computing, all your data is stored on the cloud. That's all well and good, but how secure is the cloud?

Google pushes cloud computing as safe computing—but there's really no guarantee of that. It's certainly possible that cloud systems, including Google's own servers, could be hacked and that cloud-based documents could be accessed by unauthorized users. It's also possible that third parties could hack into your own accounts and access your web-based data from your end. For that matter, it's possible that Google could experience a hardware outage that would make access to your data impossible for some period of time. (This has already happened.)

Can you trust your data to the cloud? For casual data, maybe. But if your data is highly confidential, you probably don't want to trust it with cloud computing just yet. When security matters, don't take chances—which means using a Chromebook is not right for you.

Chrome OS and Malware

Here's something else that makes the lack of local storage a good thing. Because your Chromebook can't download, store, or run traditional applications, that also means it can't download malware. At all.

With a Chromebook, unlike any other form of personal computer, there's absolutely zero chance you'll run into computer viruses, spyware, and the like. Apple may talk about having less malware than Windows, but you can still hack into the Mac OS. You simply can't hack into Chrome OS; there's nothing on your Chromebook to infect.

So with a Chromebook, you *don't* have to do any of the following:

- Install an antivirus program

- Install an anti-spyware program

- Install a firewall program

None of these items is necessary with a Chromebook because most Chromebook can't download and run malware programs. In fact, most Chromebooks can't download executable programs of any type, so you're extremely safe from this sort of attack. There are no viruses, spyware, or other infiltrations possible with the Chrome OS.

Bottom line: There's no safer computer out there than a Chromebook.

Protecting Against Phishing

Although Chrome OS and your Chromebook are, by design, virtually invulnerable to malware-based attacks, there's still the issue of those intrusions that depend on the human element to succeed. That is, when it comes to online scams, your Chromebook can't protect you from yourself.

One of the most common forms of online scams involves something called *phishing*, where a fraudster tries to extract valuable information from you via a series of fake email messages and websites.

Most phishing scams start with an email message. A phishing email is designed to look like an official email, but is in reality a clever forgery, down to the use of the original firm's logo. The goal of the email is to get you to click an enclosed link that purports to take you to an "official" website. That website, however, is also fake. Any information you provide to that website is then used for various types of fraud, from simple user name/password theft to credit card and identity theft.

For example, one common phishing scam starts with an email message that looks like it came from your bank. It's a very official-looking email, complete with the bank's logo, and it alerts you to a potential problem with your account. You're urged to click the link in the email to log into your account on the bank's website to correct the problem.

The thing is, the email itself is fraudulent, as is the site you link to. Oh, the site looks like your bank's site, but it isn't. So when you enter your username and password, or maybe even your account number, that information goes directly to the criminals behind the scam. Said criminals now have everything they need to log into your bank account and withdraw your funds into their hands. You've been scammed.

As I said, there's little Google can do to protect you from yourself; the best defense against phishing scams is simple common sense. That is, you should never click through a link in an email message that asks for any type of per-sonal information—whether that be your bank account number or eBay password or whatever. Even if the email *looks* official, it probably isn't; legiti-mate institutions and websites never include this kind of link in their official messages. If you don't click to the phishing site, you're safe.

It's Not All Good

Don't Click That Link!

If you receive an official-looking email that urges you to click a link to log into an account, don't do it. Instead, go to the website in question manu-ally, by entering the site's URL into the Chrome browser's Omnibox. After you've logged in in this fashion, you can check to see if there is any issue you need to address; if the original email was a phishing email, you'll find that everything is fine with your account. By accessing the real website manually, you've avoided falling into the phishing trap.

That said, a lot of people do click the links found in phishing emails, and pro-ceed to fraudulent websites. Because these phishing sites are designed to look like official sites, it's often difficult to tell a fraudulent site from the real thing.

Fortunately, Google Chrome includes anti-phishing technology that can detect most phishing websites. If you navigate to a known phishing website, Chrome displays a warning message instead of the suspect web page. When you see this warning message in the Chrome browser, navigate away from the troublesome web page as quickly as possible.

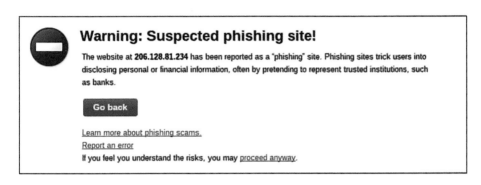

Practicing Safe Computing

As noted, Chrome includes some built-in safeguards, as well as the general benefit that comes from having limited local storage, that protects you from malware and other automated forms of computer attack. But malware isn't the only danger lurking online; you also need to defend against identity theft, cyberstalkers, and threats to your children online.

Protecting Your Personal Data

Identity thieves look to steal your personal data and then use it for their own nefarious benefit—typically by siphoning funds from your bank or credit card accounts. Fortunately, there are several steps you can take to keep your personal data safe online, including the following:

- **Always use passwords.** Make sure your Google Account has a strong password, and that every user of your Chromebook has his or her own Google Account. Don't let other users log on using your account; if you do so, they can access your files and programs, and maybe even your passwords to various sites. Restricting each user to his or her own password-protected user account puts a strong layer of protection between your data and potential thieves.

- **Create strong passwords.** Speaking of passwords, it's important that you use passwords whenever possible; do not leave any important account not password-protected. It's also important to create strong and hard-to-guess passwords; don't use common identifiers, such as your birth date or the last four digits of your Social Security number. Create as long a password as you can, using a mix of letters and numbers. Make the password as nonsensical as you can while still being able to remember it; it should not be a simple password to guess. And, to make an even stronger password, increase the length of the password; eight characters is better than six, and way better than four. You should also use a combination of letters, numbers, and special characters (!@#$%). Avoid using real words you might find in a typical dictionary; any standard dictionary cracker will crack that password faster than it takes you to type it. Also, don't use easily guessed words, like your middle name or your wife's maiden name or the name of your dog or cat. Better to use nonsense words, or random combinations or letters and numbers—anything that won't be found in a dictionary.

- **Never share passwords.** It's important to remember that your passwords should never be shared—with anyone. As blatantly obvious as that sounds, many people feel no compunction about providing others with their passwords, for whatever reason. This is a huge security risk; your password is yours and yours alone, and should never be shared or compromised.

It's Not All Good

Social Engineering

The practice of gaining access to passwords by gaining the trust of the user is called *social engineering*. This might take the form of a phone call or email from someone purporting to be from your Internet Service Provider (ISP) or company's IT department, asking you to confirm your user ID and password. When you reply, the budding social engineer on the other end of the line now has the information he needs to directly access your computer. For this reason, you should *never* give out your password, no matter how official-sounding the request.

- **Don't click unsolicited links.** As noted previously, you should never click links sent to you via email or instant messaging, if they're sent from someone you know; some Windows and Mac-based viruses hijack other users' email programs and replicate themselves via bulk email mailings.

- **Avoid entering personal information.** To better protect yourself against identity theft, you need to browse smartly and securely. It's all too easy to send personal information over the Web; if you do so cavalierly, your data could eventually end up in the hands of ID thieves. For this reason, you want to avoid entering personal information into web forms on sites with which you're not familiar. And, when shopping or providing personal information online, look for the "lock" icon on Chrome's status bar; this ensures that information is sent and received in a secure fashion.

Avoiding Cyberstalkers

You also need to protect yourself against individuals who may stalk you or your family online. These so-called *cyberstalkers* and *cyberbullies* may follow you on social networks and message forums, taunting you and leaving threatening or obscene messages. The best way to protect against cyberstalkers is to, as much as possible, hide your identity online. If the cyberstalker doesn't know who you are, he can't stalk you.

To help create a safe and relatively anonymous identity online, here are some preventative measures you should take:

- Don't share personal information online—especially with strangers in chat rooms, message forums, and social networks.

- Don't fill out public profiles on websites, blogs, and social networks—or if you do, make sure the profile doesn't contain any personal information about you (your real name, location, phone number, and so on).

- Use a gender-neutral screen name and email address.

- Avoid making a provocative statement with your screen name and email address; don't deliberately invite controversy.

- Don't flirt with other users online; avoid sexually suggestive comments.

- Don't start arguments online; don't flame other users.

Protecting Your Children Online

It's one thing to protect yourself from cyberstalkers; you also need to protect your children from online predators. Unfortunately, you can't control what your children do 24/7; you have to give them some autonomy, and with that autonomy comes the freedom to make bad decisions.

That said, there are some steps you can take to protect your children online. Here are some of the most effective things you can do:

- Take an interest in your children's online pals, just as you (should) do with friends that your kids bring home to visit.

- Talk to your children about the dangers of getting together with someone they meet online.

- Provide your children with online pseudonyms, so they don't have to use their real names online. Their online screen names should be neutral in terms of revealing gender or age.

- Forbid your children to physically meet anyone they talk to online. (This includes talking to them on the phone.)

- If you do allow your children to set up a real-world meeting, accompany them to the meeting and introduce yourself to the new friend.

- Make sure your children know that people aren't always who they pretend to be online; explain that some people view online chatting as a kind of game, where they can assume different identities.

- Set reasonable rules and guidelines for your kids' computer use; consider limiting the number of minutes/hours they can spend online each day.

- Monitor your children's Internet activities; ask them to keep a log of all websites they visit; oversee any chat and instant messaging sessions they participate in; check out any files they download; even consider sharing an email account (especially with younger children) so that you can oversee their messages.

- Instruct your children not to respond to messages that are suggestive, obscene, belligerent, or threatening, or that make them feel uncomfortable in any way; encourage your children to tell you if they receive any such messages, and then report the senders to your ISP.

- Don't let your children send pictures of themselves over the Internet; don't let them receive pictures from others. The same goes for posting personal photos on Facebook and other social networks; younger children, especially, should be discouraged from doing this.

- Caution your children about providing personal information (including passwords!) to strangers.

- Discourage your children from posting their phone numbers and other personal information on their Facebook and Twitter accounts.

- Instruct your children to only add people as Facebook friends and Twitter followers whom they know in real life; they should reject friend requests from total strangers.

- On any social networking site, set your children's privacy settings so that people can only be added as a friend if your child approves it, and so that people can only view your child's profile if they have been approved as a friend.

- As much as your children won't like it, you should occasionally check out their Facebook and Twitter feeds; look not only for any personal information they may have posted online, but also for signs of inappropriate or suspicious behavior.

- Teach your children not to respond if they receive offensive or suggestive email or instant messages.

- Use the Internet with your children; make going online a family activity.

- Consider moving the Chromebook your children use into a public room (such as a living room or den), rather than a private bedroom.

- If you think that one of your children, or one of your children's friends, is in any danger, immediately contact the authorities.

Above all, teach your children that Internet access is not a right; it should be a privilege earned by your children, and kept only when their use of it matches your expectations.

Configuring Chrome's Privacy and Security Settings

Your Chromebook includes several settings you can use to increase your online privacy and offline security.

Don't Save Passwords

By default, Chrome offers to save the passwords you use to log onto various websites. However, if another user logs onto your Chromebook using your Google Account, that person can access these password-protected sites without your knowledge or permission. It's safer, then, to *not* have Chrome save passwords.

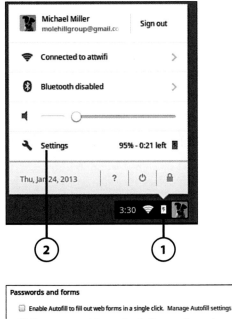

1. Click anywhere in the status area to display the Settings panel.

2. Click Settings to display the Settings page.

3. Click Show Advanced Settings and then go to the Passwords and Forms section and uncheck the Offer to Save Passwords I Enter on the Web option.

Don't Use Autofill

Similarly, Chrome's Autofill feature automatically saves the personal data you enter into web forms for later automatic entry. If you want to be sure that other unauthorized users don't have access to this web form data, you need to turn off the Autofill feature.

1. Click anywhere in the status area to display the Settings panel.

2. Click Settings to display the Settings page.

3. Click Show Advanced Settings and then go to the Passwords and Forms section and uncheck the Enable Autofill to Fill Out Web Forms in a Single Click option.

Michael Miller
molehillgroup@gmail.c   Sign out

Connected to attwifi   >

Bluetooth disabled   >

Settings   95% - 0:21 left

Thu, Jan 24, 2013   ?   ⏻   🔒

3:30

Passwords and forms

Enable Autofill to fill out web forms in a single click. Manage Autofill settings

Offer to save passwords I enter on the web. Manage saved passwords

Configure Privacy Settings

Chrome OS includes a bevy of small but important privacy settings you can configure to increase your online privacy, which are detailed in the following table.

Google Chrome Privacy Settings

Setting	Description	Recommendation
Use a web service to help resolve navigation errors.	When enabled, Google suggests alternative pages if you encounter an incorrect or nonworking URL.	When enabled, this feature sends every URL you enter to Google, where it could be stored and used for other purposes. Google doesn't need to do this, and you can figure out your own errors; for increased privacy, disable this setting.

Setting	Description	Recommendation
Use a prediction service to help complete searches and URLs typed in the address bar.	By default, Google suggests queries when you start typing a search into Chrome's Omnibox.	Because this feature sends a detailed history of your web searching to Google, you can increase your privacy by disabling this setting—and not letting Google track your search behavior.
Predict network actions to improve page load performance.	When enabled, Google "prefetches" all the URLs on each web page you load, essentially looking them up in advance in the event you click them. This should speed up the loading of any subsequent pages you click to.	This is a fairly harmless option, at least in terms of privacy. Because it can, in theory, speed up your browsing, it's a good option to enable.
	Google's anti-phishing protection works by comparing the URLs you enter with a database of known phishing URLs.	Although Chrome might send some subset of the URL you enter to Google, Google never sees the full URL, and doesn't track your browsing history. Because of the valuable protection offered, this is a good feature to keep enabled.
Use a web service to help resolve spelling errors.	This adds spell checking to Chrome, using the same spell-checking technology employed by Google search.	When this option is enabled, anything you type into the Chrome browser is sent to Google's servers for evaluation. Not only can this slow down your browsing, it's also sending more personal data to Google. Best not to enable it.
Automatically send usage statistics and crash reports to Google.	By default, Google receives reports about how you use Chrome and what you're doing if and when the browser crashes.	Usage statistics and crash reports? That means Google receives a copy of everything you do in Chrome. You can increase your privacy by disabling this setting and not letting Google track all your actions.
Send a "Do Not Track" request with your browsing traffic.	This technology lets you opt out of tracking by websites you don't actually visit—advertising networks, analytic services, and the like.	When you enable this option, you get fewer entities tracking your web browsing—which is a good thing, privacy-wise.

1. Click anywhere in the status area to display the Settings panel.

2. Click Settings to display the Settings page.

3. Click Show Advanced Settings and then go to the Privacy section and uncheck any settings you don't want to use.

Configure Content Settings

Chrome also includes a half-dozen settings that determine what content is displayed in the browser. The following table details these settings.

Google Chrome Content Settings

Setting	Description	Recommendation
Cookies	Cookies are small files that websites store on your computer to track your browsing behavior. You can opt to allow cookies (default) or block all cookies. You can also allow cookies except from third-party sites or clear cookies when you close your browser.	As onerous as cookies sound, they help make it easier to revisit your favorite sites. However, you can increase your privacy by blocking all cookies, or by clearing cookies when you close your browser (log off from Chrome). Know, however, that without cookies, you'll need to re-enter all your personal data each time you visit a website.
Images	You can opt to show all images on web pages, or not show any images.	Not showing images speeds up web browsing, but decreases the usability of many sites.
JavaScript	JavaScript is a kind of programming language used to create certain website content. Unfortunately, JavaScript can be used to run malicious scripts in your browser—although that's much less likely or dangerous in the Chrome OS.	Although you can increase security by not running JavaScript, this can make some websites less functional. Because Chrome OS is fairly protected against malicious code, this setting is probably safe to leave enabled.
Plug-ins	You can increase the functionality of your browser, and of certain websites, by running plug-in software.	Most plug-ins are harmless. If you're concerned about security, you can disable this setting—although some sites might not run as advertised.
Pop-ups	Pop-up windows are a particularly pernicious form of unwanted online advertising. Most people hate them.	You can make your web browsing less annoying by letting Chrome block all pop-ups. (This is the default setting.)
Location	Some websites can serve up a more personalized experience if they know where you're located.	Do you really want all the sites you visit to know where you're at? You can increase your privacy by turning off location tracking, or at least forcing sites to ask you before they track.

1. Click anywhere in the status area to display the Settings panel.

2. Click Settings to display the Settings page.

3. Click Show Advanced Settings and then go to the Privacy section and click the Content Settings button.

4. When the Content Settings page appears, select or deselect the desired settings.

5. Click OK.

Clear Browsing Data

If you want to cover your tracks, as it were, you can clear the data that Chrome keeps about your browsing history. In particular, you can do the following:

- Clear browsing history

- Clear download history

- Empty the cache

- Delete cookies and other site data

- Clear saved passwords

- Clear saved Autofill form data

1. Click anywhere in the status area to display the Settings panel.

2. Click Settings to display the Settings page.

3. Click Show Advanced Settings and then go to the Privacy section and click the Clear Browsing Data button.

4. When the Clear Browsing Data dialog box appears, check those items you want to clear or delete.

5. Pull down the list and select how much data (for how long) you want to clear.

6. Click the Clear Browsing Data button.

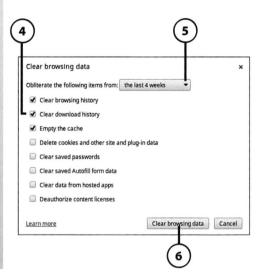

Restrict Sign-In

There's one last setting you should consider. By default, anyone with a Google Account can log into your Chromebook and then into their own personal data and settings. You might not want just anyone to use your Chromebook, however; to that end, you (as your Chromebook's owner) can limit use to only those people you pre select.

1. Click anywhere in the status area to display the Settings panel.

2. Click Settings to display the Settings page.

3. Go to the Users section and click the Manage Other Users button.

4. Check the Restrict Sign-In to the Following Users option.

5. Enter the email addresses of those people you want to be able to use your Chromebook into the Add Users box and then press Enter.

6. To remove someone from the approved user list, click the X next to his or her name.

7. Click the OK button.

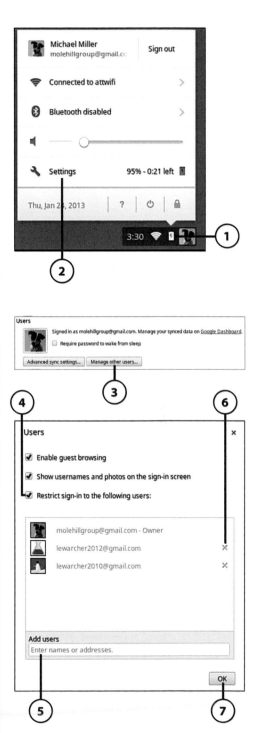

In this chapter, you find out how to get the most from your Chromebook.

→ Optimizing Battery Life
→ Speeding Up Performance

Optimizing Your Chromebook's Performance

Out of the box, a Chromebook is a very fast computer with a long battery life. There are things you can do, however, to make it run even faster—and last longer on a charge.

Optimizing Battery Life

Let's start with your Chromebook's battery life. On average, you're going to get 4 to 6 hours per charge, depending on the model, which is pretty good. Your battery might last longer, however, if you take the appropriate precautions.

Use the Right Adapter

Use only the charger/adapter supplied by your Chromebook's manufacturer, or an authorized replacement. Using the wrong charger/adapter can negatively affect the life of your battery—or even damage the Chromebook itself.

Keep It Cool

Batteries don't like heat. The hotter the room, the less the battery will hold its charge—and the increased likelihood you'll damage the Chromebook. Worst-case scenario, your Chromebook will get hot enough to catch fire. This is not desirable.

It's best, then, to keep your Chromebook as near room temperature as possible, even when it's not in use.

Keep a Little Charge

When you're not using your Chromebook for an extended period, charge the battery to about the 30% or 40% level. This level of charge maintains battery performance as best possible.

Dim the Screen

When running on battery power, turn down your Chromebook's screen brightness. A brighter screen draws more power, and runs the battery down faster.

Disable Wireless

If you're not working online, turn off either or both Wi-Fi and 3G wireless functionality. (Not all Chromebooks offer 3G, of course.) Your Chromebook's wireless receiver draws a lot of power.

Of course, your Chromebook is fairly useless if not connected to the Internet, so this might not be a viable option. If you have an Ethernet connection, however, you can use that and turn off the wireless function.

Disk Use

On a traditional notebook computer, you are advised to minimize the use of your hard disk and optical disk (DVD) to maximize battery life. Because your Chromebook doesn't have a DVD drive (and most don't have hard drives), this advice doesn't translate.

>>>Go Further

BATTERY REPLACEMENT

All batteries get weaker over time. If your battery life starts to deteriorate, or if your battery stops working altogether, you need to replace it with a new battery.

Unfortunately, the battery is sealed into your Chromebook; it's not user replaceable. To remove or replace your Chromebook's internal battery, you need to take it or send it to an authorized service center.

Speeding Up Performance

On a traditional computer, you can speed up performance by managing how programs use the PC's memory and hard disk. Because most Chromebooks don't have hard disks, there isn't much to manage there—which is one of the reasons a Chromebook is so fast by default.

There are a few things you can do, however, to speed up the performance of your Chromebook. Because most of what you do will be web-based, most of these tricks involve how you browse online.

Don't Multitask

Each web app that's running takes up processor capacity, memory, and upload/download bandwidth. If you have multiple apps running simultaneously, in multiple browser tabs or windows, that can really slow down your Chromebook's processing—and clog up your Internet connection.

This can even be the case if some of those apps are running in the background, like a real-time weather or stock app. Bottom line, if you don't want your Chromebook to become too sluggish, close some of those browser tabs.

Disable or Remove Extensions

Similarly, the Chrome extensions you install can create a drain on your memory and processing power. The more little buttons you have on the Chrome toolbar, the more things your Chromebook has to run. Speed things up by disabling or removing those extensions you don't really need or use, as discussed in Chapter 11, "Using Chrome Apps and Extensions."

Enable DNS Prefetching

When configured properly, the Chrome browser can "prefetch" all the URLs on each web page you load, essentially looking them up in advance in the event you click them. This speeds up the loading of any subsequent pages you click to, which results in faster browsing.

1. From within the Chrome browser, click the Customize and Control button to display the drop-down menu.

2. Click Settings.

3. When the Settings page appears, click Show Advanced Settings and then go to the Privacy section and check the Predict Network Actions to Improve Page Load Performance option.

New tab	Ctrl+T
New window	Ctrl+N
New incognito window	Ctrl+Shift+N
Bookmarks	▶

| Edit | Cut | Copy | Paste |

Save page as...	Ctrl+S
Find...	Ctrl+F
Print...	Ctrl+P

| Zoom | − 100% + | ⌜⌟ |

| History | Ctrl+H |
| Downloads | Ctrl+J |

| Settings |
| Report an issue... |
| More tools | ▶ |

Privacy

Content settings...   Clear browsing data...

Google Chrome may use web services to improve your browsing experience. You may optionally disable these services. Learn more

☑ Use a web service to help resolve navigation errors
☑ Use a prediction service to help complete searches and URLs typed in the address bar
☑ Predict network actions to improve page load performance
☑ Enable phishing and malware protection
☐ Use a web service to help resolve spelling errors
☑ Automatically send usage statistics and crash reports to Google
☐ Send a 'Do Not Track' request with your browsing traffic

Disable Feedback to Google

There are several configuration settings that send information to Google for further action. Forgetting for the moment the privacy implications of these operations, they can slow down your web browsing—especially if you're on a slow connection. Data you send upstream to Google can clog up the pipeline for the data you need to flow downstream.

1. From within the Chrome browser, click the Customize and Control button to display the drop-down menu.

2. Click Settings.

3. When the Settings page appears, click Show Advanced Settings, and then go to the Privacy section and uncheck the following options:

   - Use a web service to help resolve navigation errors

   - Use a prediction service to help complete searches and URLs typed into the address bar

   - Automatically send usage statistics and crash reports to Google

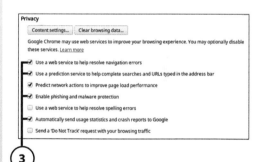

It's Not All Good

Performance Versus Protection

Another way to (slightly) speed up your Chromebook's browsing performance is to disable Chrome's phishing and malware protection. Unfortunately, doing so removes important protection against phishing sites. For that reason, it's recommended that you leave this option enabled.

Chrome's Task
Manager

Task Manager - Google Chrome				✕

Task	Private m...	CPU ▼	Network	FPS
● ◎ Browser	69,896K	3	0	N/A
● ✷ GPU Process	55,840K	2	N/A	N/A
● ✷ Web Worker: https://docs.google.com/fe/s/fe.s.C	40,928K	0	N/A	N/A
● ✷ Plug-in Broker: Shockwave Flash	3,900K	0	N/A	N/A
● ✷ Plug-in: Google Talk Plugin	3,472K	0	N/A	N/A
● ✷ Plug-in: Shockwave Flash	7,284K	0	N/A	N/A
● ✷ Background Page: TweetDeck	9,280K	0	0	N/A
● ⑧ Tab: Google	25,732K	0	0	0
● ✷ Background Page: Google Drive	18,896K	0	0	0

Stats for nerds   End process

In this chapter, you find out how to deal with any potential problems you may encounter with your Chromebook.

→ Dealing with a Frozen App or Web Page
→ Resetting Your Chromebook
→ Recovering from Severe Problems
→ Updating Chrome OS

Troubleshooting and Recovering from Problems

Your Chromebook is much more reliable than a traditional personal computer. The lack of any moving parts (no hard drive or optical drive) enhances reliability, and the technical compactness of Chrome OS (no legacy stuff to support) means there's less stuff to go wrong.

That doesn't mean you'll never encounter any problems, however; there are still times when a particular app or web page or even your entire Chromebook might freeze. Fortunately, your Chromebook's inherent simplicity makes it easy to troubleshoot and recover from even the most significant issues.

Dealing with a Frozen App or Web Page

Perhaps the most common problem you're likely to encounter is a frozen application or web page—that is, the tab you're currently on doesn't respond to anything you do. Sometimes you can navigate off this tab to another tab or window, sometimes not, but in any case you're left with one nonresponsive tab.

When this happens, you can undertake the following steps, in order, to close the tab and resume your other work:

1. Start by simply trying to close the tab. Click the X on the tab itself, or select the tab and then press Ctrl+W (or do both).

2. If the tab is still frozen, you can try shutting down the window it's in by pressing Ctrl+Shift+W. (This only works if you have more than one window open.)

3. If that doesn't work, press Shift+Esc (or click the Customize and Control button and select More Tools, Task Manager) to open the Chrome Task Manager. All running tasks (apps, pages, extensions, and so forth) are listed in the Task Manager window. To close the frozen task, click that task and then click the End Process button.

Task Manager

Chrome OS features a Task Manager, similar to the one in Microsoft Windows. You use the Task Manager to review all running tasks and services—and to shut down tasks that won't close of their own accord.

4. If the tab still won't close, you need to shut down and then restart your Chromebook. Press and hold the Power button for about 8 seconds until your Chromebook completely powers off—then restart your Chromebook and get back to work.

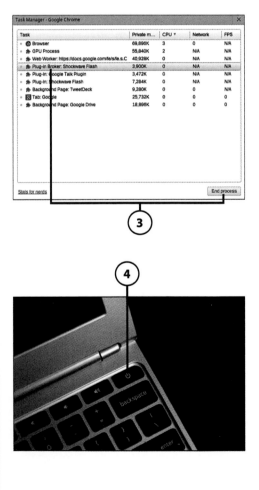

Resetting Your Chromebook

Although most of the data you use on your Chromebook are stored in the cloud, some personal data (primarily about user accounts) are stored locally. Sometimes this locally stored data can become corrupted, causing your Chromebook to misbehave.

When this happens, you can often get things working again by resetting your Chromebook to its original condition. This in effect clears all your local data from the Chromebook, leaving you with a factory-fresh machine.

It's Not All Good

When you reset your Chromebook, you not only clear usernames and logon information, you also delete any other data saved on your Chromebook. This includes photos, downloaded files, saved networks, and the like. All data for all accounts is deleted. The next time you start up your Chromebook will be just like the first time; you'll be prompted to create a new user account, and so forth.

1. Click anywhere in the status area to display the Settings panel.

2. Click Settings to display the Settings page.

3. Scroll to the bottom of the page and click Show Advanced Settings.

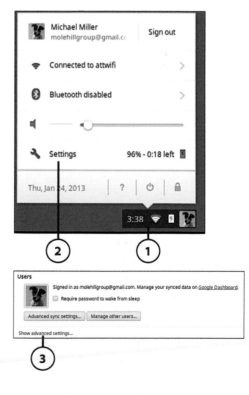

4. Go to the Factory Reset section and then click the Reset button.

5. Click the Restart button in the Factory Reset dialog box.

    This restarts your Chromebook, with all local data deleted. Follow the instructions in Chapter 1, "Unboxing and Setting Up Your Chromebook," to create a new user account and set up your Chromebook from scratch.

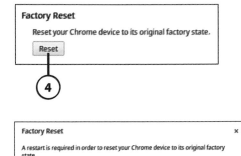

Reset from the Sign-In Screen

You can also reset your Chromebook from the sign-in screen. Just press Ctrl+Alt+Shift+R and then click Restart.

Recovering from Severe Problems

Some Chromebook problems are not so easy to recover from. If your Chromebook constantly freezes or otherwise exhibits significant chronic problems, you might need to wipe the current version of Chrome OS from your machine and reinstall the operating system from scratch.

Reinstalling Chrome OS on your Chromebook is called the *recovery process*, because you have to recover the operating system from a system image you save to an external USB storage device. To create this recovery drive, you must have access to a Windows, Mac, or Linux computer to which you have administrative privileges; you also need a USB flash drive with at least 4GB of free space.

It's Not All Good

Because of the technical complexity involved, you should attempt the recovery process only in extreme situations, and if you're technically comfortable and competent to proceed. Note that the recovery process deletes all user information and data files saved on your Chromebook, including photos, downloaded files, saved networks, and the like. When you restart your Chromebook after the recovery, it will be just like the first time; you'll be prompted to create a new user account, and so forth.

1. On your non-Chromebook computer, insert a blank USB flash drive, and then open your web browser and go to https://dl.google.com/dl/chromeos/recovery/chromeos-imagecreator.exe.

2. Download and run the chromeosimagecreator.exe file and then follow the onscreen instructions to run the recovery tool and create a recovery flash drive.

3. On your Chromebook, press the Power button for 8 seconds to power off.

4. Insert the recovery flash drive into your Chromebook's USB port.

5. Insert one end of a paper clip into the small hole on the bottom of your Chromebook. (Different manufacturers may place this recovery hole in different places; on the Samsung Chromebook, it's pretty much in the middle of the unit.)

6. Hold the paperclip in this hole while you press the Power button to power on your Chromebook.

7. When you see the Chrome OS Is Missing or Damaged screen, follow the onscreen instructions to update your Chromebook's system.

8. When your Chromebook restarts, remove the USB recovery drive.

    This restarts your Chromebook, with the operating system reinstalled. Follow the instructions in Chapter 1 to create a new user account and set up your Chromebook from scratch.

Updating Chrome OS

One of the nice things about Chrome OS is that it automatically updates itself every time it's turned on. That is, when you power up your Chromebook, Chrome goes online to check for updates; if any are available, they're automatically downloaded and installed.

If Chrome detects a new update while you're using your Chromebook, you can manually update Chrome OS without waiting for the next time you shut down and then restart your machine. If an update is available, a special version of the Customize and Control (wrench) icon appears.

1. Click anywhere in the status area to display the Settings pane.

2. Select Restart to Update.

   Chrome now downloads the update and restarts your Chromebook. Log back in as normal to resume work.

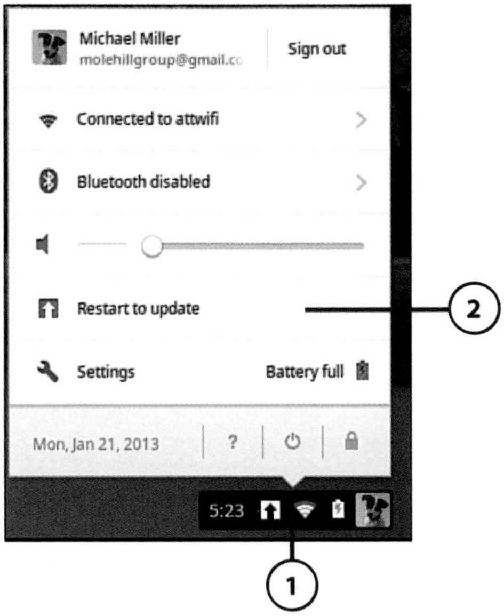

	Michael Miller molehillgroup@gmail.co	Sign out
🛜	Connected to attwifi	>
🅱	Bluetooth disabled	>
🔇	⬤	
↑	Restart to update	——— ②
🔧	Settings	Battery full 🔋
Mon, Jan 21, 2013	? ⏻ 🔒	

5:23 ↑ 🛜 🔋 👤

①

A

Google Chrome Keyboard Shortcuts

A keyboard shortcut is a combination of two or more keyboard buttons that you use to perform specific actions within Google Chrome. Using keyboard shortcuts can be a real time saver.

Navigation and Browser Shortcuts

Keyboard Shortcut	Action
Ctrl+Alt+/	Display list of keyboard shortcuts
Ctrl+o	Open a file
Ctrl+m	Open File Manager
Shift+Esc	Open Task Manager
Ctrl+h	Open History page
Ctrl+j	Open Downloads page
Alt+e	Open Customize and Control menu
Ctrl+Shift+b	Toggle Bookmarks bar on or off
Ctrl+Full Screen	Configure external monitor
Ctrl+Alt+z	Enable/disable accessibility settings (if you're not logged into a Google Account)
Ctrl+Shift+q	Sign out of your Google Account
Ctrl+?	Go to Help Center

Tab and Window Navigation Shortcuts

Keyboard Shortcut	Action
Ctrl+t	Open a new tab
Ctrl+w	Close the current tab
Ctrl+Shift+t	Reopen the last tab you closed
Ctrl+Tab	Go to next tab
Ctrl+Shift+Tab	Go to previous tab
Ctrl+1 through Ctrl+8	Go to the specified tab
Ctrl+9	Go to the last tab
Ctrl+n	Open a new window
Ctrl+Shift+n	Open a new window in Incognito mode
Ctrl+Shift+w	Close the current window
Alt+Tab	Go to next window
Alt+Shift+Tab	Go to previous window
Alt+1 through Alt+8	Go to the specified window
Alt+9	Go to the last open window
Alt+-	Minimize window
Alt+=	Maximize window
Alt+Shift and +	Center current window
Click and hold Back or Forward button in browser toolbar	See browsing history for that tab
Backspace or Alt+Left Arrow	Go to previous page in browsing history
Shift+Backspace or Alt+Right Arrow	Go to next page in browsing history
Ctrl+click a link	Open link in new tab in background
Ctrl+Shift+click a link	Open link in new tab in foreground
Shift+click a link	Open link in new window
Drag a link to a tab	Open link in the tab
Drag a link to a blank area on the tab strip	Open link in new tab
Type URL in Address bar; then press Alt+Enter	Open URL in new tab
Press Esc while dragging a tab	Return tab to its original position

Page Shortcuts

Keyboard Shortcut	Description
Alt+Up Arrow	Page up
Alt+Down Arrow	Page down
Space bar	Scroll down web page
Ctrl+Alt+Up Arrow	Home
Ctrl+Alt+Down Arrow	End
Ctrl+p	Print page
Ctrl+s	Save page
Ctrl+r	Reload page
Ctrl+Shift+r	Reload page without using cached content
Esc	Stop loading current page
Ctrl and +	Zoom in
Ctrl and -	Zoom out
Ctrl+0	Reset zoom level
Ctrl+d	Save page as bookmark
Ctrl+Shift+d	Save all open pages in window as bookmarks in a new folder
Drag a link to Bookmarks bar	Save link as bookmark
Ctrl+f	Search current page
Ctrl+g or Enter	Go to next match for page search
Ctrl+Shift+g or Shift+Enter	Go to previous match for page search
Ctrl+k or Ctrl+e	Search web
Ctrl+Enter	Add www. and .com to input in Address bar and open resulting URL
Ctrl+Next Window	Take a screenshot of current screen
Ctrl+u	View page source
Ctrl+Shift+i	Toggle display of Developer Tools panel
Ctrl+Shift+j	Toggle display of the DOM Inspector

Text Editing Shortcuts

Keyboard Shortcut	Description
Ctrl+a	Select everything on page
Ctrl+l or Alt+d	Select content in Omnibar
Ctrl+Shift+Right Arrow	Select next word or letter
Ctrl+Shift+Left Arrow	Select previous word or letter
Ctrl+Right Arrow	Move to start of next word
Ctrl+Left Arrow	Move to start of previous word
Ctrl+c	Copy selected content to clipboard
Ctrl+v	Paste content from clipboard
Ctrl+Shift+v	Paste content from clipboard as plain text
Ctrl+x	Cut
Ctrl+Backspace	Delete previous word
Alt+Backspace	Delete next letter
Ctrl+z	Undo last action

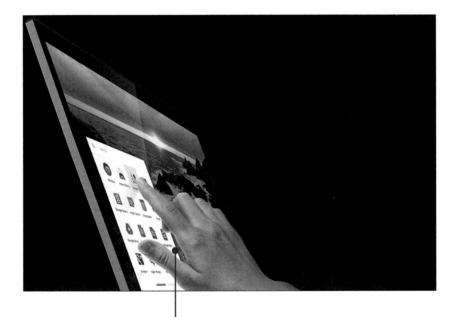

Chromebook Pixel
display

In this appendix, you learn about Google's newest Chromebook, the Chromebook Pixel.

→ Introducing the Chromebook Pixel
→ Who Needs a $1,299 Chromebook?

B

Google Chromebook Pixel

Whereas other Chromebooks are manufactured (often to Google's specs) and sold by traditional computer hardware manufacturers, Google is selling one very special Chromebook under its own brand. This new machine is dubbed the Chromebook Pixel, and it's a high-end delight that competes with pricey ultrabooks and hybrids from the like of Apple and Microsoft.

Introducing the Chromebook Pixel

Google's Chromebook Pixel is a state-of-the-art ultrabook computer that happens to run the Chrome operating system. It competes head-to-head with other high-end ultrabooks—and bests them, in many performance categories.

Like most other Chromebooks, the Pixel is a web-based computer. That is, there's no internal hard disk or CD/DVD drive; it runs programs and stores files in the cloud, not locally. As such it's relatively small and lightweight, and has very good battery life.

Google Chromebook Pixel

What makes the Pixel different from other Chromebooks is the hardware. Instead of a standard "Chiclet" keyboard, it features a pretty cool backlit keyboard that lights up for nighttime computing. The touchpad is made from etched glass for smooth control and enhanced accuracy. And the overall build is more solid than you get on a sub-$300 unit.

The best part of the Pixel, though, and where it gets its name, is the display. The Pixel features an ultra-high resolution 12.85" screen—both larger and sharper than other Chromebook displays. The Pixel screen contains 4.3 million individual pixels, for a pixel density of 239 pixels/inch. Compare that with the 118 pixels/inch density for most notebook computers, and what you get is crisper text, more detailed backgrounds, and more vivid colors.

The Pixel also boasts a touchscreen display. That means you can operate some applications just by tapping or dragging across the screen with your finger. The display is covered by a thin layer of Gorilla Glass, to reduce wear and tear. (And breakage!)

Gorilla Glass
Gorilla Glass is a special kind of glass, manufactured by Corning, that is more damage-resistant than normal glass. It's used in a lot of high-tech devices, including Apple's iPhone and other smartphones and tablets.

The Pixel's display also has a 3:2 screen ratio, compared to the normal 16:9 or 16:10 ratio found on most notebooks. Google calls it the "photographic format," and it's definitely a different experience than the widescreen displays that are ubiquitous today.

And there's more. The Pixel boasts a faster processor than that found in other Chromebooks, a 1.8Ghz dual-core Intel i5, which is similar to what you find in high-end Mac and Windows ultrabooks. You also get 4GB of RAM and 32GB of solid-state storage, which is more than what you get in competing Chromebooks.

All of this makes the Pixel a very unique Chromebook. It's also a very expensive one. The base model, with built-in Wi-Fi connectivity, sells for $1,299. There's also a pricier version, which adds 3G/4G cellular connectivity (and ups the internal storage to 64GB), that sells for a whopping $1,449. That's a lot more than the $249 most people are spending on Chromebooks today.

The following table details the specifications for the two Chromebook Pixel models.

Chromebook Pixel Specifications

	Chromebook Pixel (Wi-Fi)	Chromebook Pixel (Wi-Fi + LTE)
List price	$1,299.99	$1,449.99
Screen size	12.85"	12.85"
Resolution (pixels)	2560 × 1700	2560 × 1700
Dimensions	8.84" × 11.7" × 0.64"	8.84" × 11.7" × 0.64"
Weight	3.35 lbs.	2.35 lbs.
Battery life	5 hours	5 hours
Wi-Fi wireless connectivity	Yes (dual-band 802.11 a/b/g/n)	Yes (dual-band 802.11 a/b/g/n)
3G/4G LTE wireless connectivity	No	Yes
Memory	4GB	4GB
Solid state data storage	32GB	64GB
Hard drive storage	None	None
Processor	1.8GHz Dual-core Intel i5	1.8GHz Dual-core Intel i5
USB ports	2 (USB 2.0)	2 (USB 2.)
Memory card slot	2-in-1 (SD/MMC)	2-in-1 (SD/MMC)

	Chromebook Pixel (Wi-Fi)	Chromebook Pixel (Wi-Fi + LTE)
External video port(s)	Mini DisplayPort	Mini DisplayPort
Ethernet port	No	No
Built-in webcam	Yes	Yes
Webcam resolution	720p HD	720p HD
Operating system	Google Chrome OS	Google Chrome OS

Who Needs a $1,299 Chromebook?

To be honest, I can't see the average consumer taking much interest in the $1,299 Chromebook Pixel. It takes everything that the public likes about the $249 Samsung Chromebook and turns it on its ear. Yes, the hardware is nice (especially that screen!), but the price is just way, way too high. In this price range, Google is competing with full-blown ultrabooks and notebook/tablet hybrids, such as the MacBook Pro and Microsoft Surface Pro. Plus, the touch-screen on the Pixel is fairly useless, as Chrome OS isn't really a touchscreen operating system and there are few, if any, touchscreen apps developed for Chrome.

So why did Google develop the Pixel—and for whom? I tend to view the Pixel as more of a proof of concept than a viable consumer product. Everything about the Pixel is top-notch, from the backlit keyboard to the high resolution display to the glass touchpad; it's as if Google were demonstrating to the market just what could be done with a Chromebook, if you wanted to. Given that current Chromebook sales are driven by price, with the machines des-tined for use as a secondary computing device, Google certainly can't expect serious users to replace their current high-end notebooks with a web-based Chromebook, no matter how cool the hardware.

That said, the Pixel might find a niche market among tech-savvy early adopt-ers; they'll certainly be attracted to the screen. And software developers have been asking for a more rugged Chromebook on which to develop Chrome apps, so the Pixel might appeal to them. But I don't see a lot of appeal to the general public; for the masses, the $249 Samsung Chromebook is the machine to buy.

To learn more about the Chromebook Pixel, and to order one for yourself, go to www.google.com/intl/en/chrome/devices/chromebook-pixel/. It's certainly worth a look.

Index

N

O

Q

R

S

X-Z

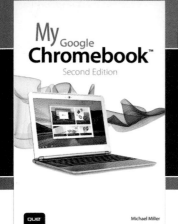

My Google Chromebook™
Second Edition

Michael Miller

que

Safari Books Online

FREE Online Edition

Your purchase of *My Google Chromebook, Second Edition* includes access to a free online edition for 45 days through the **Safari Books Online** subscription service. Nearly every Que book is available online through **Safari Books Online**, along with thousands of books and videos from publishers such as Addison-Wesley Professional, Cisco Press, Exam Cram, IBM Press, O'Reilly Media, Prentice Hall, Sams, and VMware Press.

Safari Books Online is a digital library providing searchable, on-demand access to thousands of technology, digital media, and professional development books and videos from leading publishers. With one monthly or yearly subscription price, you get unlimited access to learning tools and information on topics including mobile app and software development, tips and tricks on using your favorite gadgets, networking, project management, graphic design, and much more.

Activate your FREE Online Edition at
informit.com/safarifree

STEP 1: Enter the coupon code: GZKXDDB.

STEP 2: New Safari users, complete the brief registration form.
Safari subscribers, just log in.

If you have difficulty registering on Safari or accessing the online edition,
please e-mail customer-service@safaribooksonline.com